Pocket China
in
Figures

2015 Edition

Pocket China
in
Figures

2015 Edition

Zhichang Liu

Chinese Academy of Social Sciences, China

World Scientific

W JERSEY • LONDON • SINGAPORE • BEIJING • SHANGHAI • HONG KONG • TAIPEI • CHENNAI

Published by

World Scientific Publishing Co. Pte. Ltd.

5 Toh Tuck Link, Singapore 596224

USA office: 27 Warren Street, Suite 401-402, Hackensack, NJ 07601

UK office: 57 Shelton Street, Covent Garden, London WC2H 9HE

British Library Cataloguing-in-Publication Data
A catalogue record for this book is available from the British Library.

POCKET CHINA IN FIGURES
2015 Edition

ISBN   978-981-4644-51-8

Typeset by Stallion Press
Email: enquiries@stallionpress.com

Printed in Singapore

Contents

Part 1

China

Top-Line Indicators

About China

Area (sq. km)	9,600,000
Arable (sq. km)	1,217,200
Arable as % of Total Land	12.8
Average Temperature (°C)	10.2
Total Rainfall (mm)	653.5
Capital	Beijing
Currency	Yuan

Social Indicators

Population (million)	1,360.7
Pop. Per sq. km	141.7
Rate of Natural Increase (‰)	4.9
Crude Birth Rate (‰)	12.1
Crude Death Rate (‰)	7.2
Human Development Index	0.72
Life Expectancy (Census in 2010)	74.8
Men	72.4
Women	77.4
Illiterate Rate (%, 2010)	4.08%
Doctors Per 10,000 Population	5.3

Economic Indicators

Gross National Income (¥ billion)	56,613
Gross Domestic Product (¥ billion)	56,885
Gross Domestic Product ($ billion)	9,240
Real Economic Growth Rate (%)	7.7
CPI — All Items (annual percentage change)	2.6

Retail Price Index (annual percentage change)	1.4
Producer Price Index for Industrial Products (annual percentage change)	−1.9
Total External Trade (¥ billion)	258.2
Overseas Visitor Arrivals ('000)	129,078
Chinese Outbound Visitors ('000)	98,185
Total Passenger Traffic (million)	21,230
Total Cargo Handled (million tons)	40,989
Money Supply (M1) (¥ billion)	33,729
Balance of Payments ($ million)	431,379
Debt of Central Government (¥ billion)	8,675
Investment in Fixed Assets (¥ billion)	44,629
Foreign Direct Investment Actually Utilized ($ million)	117,586

Population

Population by Sex

	Million	%
Total Population at Year-end	1,360.7	100.0
Male	697.3	51.2
Female	663.4	48.8

Population by Residence

	Million	%
Urban Population	731.1	53.73
Rural Population	629.6	46.27

Population by Age

	Million	%
Aged 0–14	223.3	16.4
Aged 15–64	1,005.8	73.9
Aged 65 and Over	131.6	9.7

Population by Marital Status

	Total	Males	Females
Total (Aged 15 and Over)	100.0	100.0	100.0
Single	20.2	23.5	16.7
Married	72.8	71.3	74.4
Widowed	5.4	3.3	7.6
Divorced/Separated	1.6	1.8	1.3

Vital Rates

Crude Birth Rate (Per 1,000 Population)	12.08
Crude Death Rate (‰)	7.16
Natural Growth Rate (‰)	4.92
Total Fertility Rate (Per 1,000 Female)	35.68

Dependency Ratio of Population

	%
Gross Dependency Ratio	35.3
Children Dependency Ratio	22.2
Old Dependency Ratio	13.1

Labor Force

Principal Employment Statistics

	Million
Economically Active Population	793.0
Total Number of Employed Persons	769.8
Urban Employed Persons	382.4
Rural Employed Persons	387.4
Registered Unemployed Persons in Urban Areas	9.26
Registered Unemployment Rate in Urban Areas (%)	4.05

Employed Persons by Industry

	Million	%
Economically Active Population	793	
Total	770	100
Agriculture	242	31.4
Industry	232	30.1
Services	296	38.5

Number of Employed Persons in Urban Areas

	Million
Total	382.4
State-owned Units	63.7
Urban Collective-owned Units	5.7
Cooperative Units	1.1
Joint Ownership Units	0.3
Limited Liability Corporations	60.7
Share-holding Corporations Ltd.	17.2
Private Enterprises	82.4
Units with Funds from Hong Kong, Macao and Taiwan	14.0

Foreign Funded Units	15.7
Self-employed Individuals	61.4

Number of Employed Persons in Rural Areas

	Million
Total	387.4
Private Enterprises	42.8
Self-employed Individuals	31.9

National Income

National Income

	Yuan	Dollars
Gross National Income (billion)	56,613	9,137
GDP (billion)	56,885	9,181
Per Capita GDP	41,908	6,764

Composition of GDP

	%
Agriculture	10.0
Industry	43.9
Services	46.1

Indices of GDP

	Preceding year = 100
Gross National Income	107.4
Gross Domestic Product	107.7
Per Capita GDP	107.1

Expenditure on GDP (at Current Market Prices)

	Billion Yuan	Percentage Distribution
Total	58,667.3	100.0
Final Consumption	29,216.6	36.2
Investment	28,035.6	13.6
Net Exports	1,415.1	47.8

Balance of Payments

Balance of Payments

	Million Dollars
A — Current Account Balance	182,807
B — Capital and Financial Account Balance	326,203
C — Net Errors and Omissions	−77,631
D — Overall Balance (A + B + C)	431,379
E — Reserve Assets	−431,379

Current Account Balance

	Million Dollars
Current Account Balance	182,807
Goods and Services	235,380
Goods Balance	359,890
Exports of Goods	2,218,977
Imports of Goods	1,859,087
Services Balance	−124,510
Exports of Services	206,018
Imports of Services	330,528
Income and Profit	−43,839
Compensation of Staff and Workers	16,076
Profit from Investment	−59,915
Current Transfers	−8,733
Governments	−3,113
Other Departments	−5,621

Capital and Financial Account Balance

	Million Dollars
Capital and Financial Account Balance	326,203
Capital Account	3,052
Financial Account	323,151
Direct Investments	184,972
Securities	60,547
Other Investments	77,633

Debts of Central Government

	Billion Yuan
Total	8675
Domestic Debts	8584
External Debts	91

Investment in Fixed Assets

Actual Funds for Investment

	Billion Yuan
Total	49,161
State Budget	2,231
Domestic Loans	5,944
Foreign Investment	432
Self-raising Funds	33,428
Others	7,127

Structure of Investment

	Billion Yuan
Total	44,629.4
Construction and Installation	29,842.4
Purchase of Equipment and Instruments	9,107.4
Others	5,679.5

Structure of Investment by Industry

	Billion Yuan
Total	44,629
Agriculture	44,629
Industry	1,119
Services	18,481

Investment in China and Abroad

Foreign Direct Investment

	Number of Projects
1990	7,273
2000	22,347
2010	27,406
2011	27,712
2012	24,925
2013	22,773

Foreign Direct Investment Actually Utilized by Countries or Regions

	Million Dollars
Total	117,586.2
Hong Kong, China	73,396.7
Singapore	7,228.7
Japan	7,058.2
Virgin Islands	6,158.6
Republic of Korea	3,054.2
United States	2,819.9
Taiwan, China	2,087.7
Germany	2,078.4
Samoan	1,858.1
Cayman Islands	1,668.3
Netherlands	1,274.8
Mauritius	910.3
France	751.9
Bermuda	721.9
Canada	536.1
Thailand	483.1

Macao, China	460.2
Luxembourg	432.6
United Kingdom	391.9
Denmark	369.6
Seychelles	348.1
Australia	329.7
Italy	316.9
Switzerland	314.7
Spain	312.0
Malaysia	280.5
Sweden	208.5
Barbados	161.0
Austria	153.4
Brunei	133.2
Indonesia	126.2
Finland	89.6
Bahamas	81.9
New Zealand	68.0
Philippines	67.3
Saudi Arabia	58.5
Marshall Islands	48.8
United Arab Emirates	43.8
Ireland	43.2
Belize	42.0
Turkey	40.0
Uganda	35.8
Belgium	34.5
Norway	27.9
India	27.1
Panama	25.9
Brazil	23.0
Cambodia	22.5
Russia	22.1

Cyprus	21.3
Chile	20.9
Pakistan	18.1
Qatar	17.7
Tanzania	16.3
Namibia	16.0
Mexico	15.8
Nigeria	14.9
Zambia	14.9
Israel	13.7
South Africa	12.9
Czech	11.0

Foreign Direct Investment by Industry

	Million Dollars
Total	117,586
Agriculture, Forestry, Animal Husbandry and Fishery	1,800
Mining	365
Manufacturing	45,555
Production and Supply of Electricity, Gas and Water	2,429
Construction	1,220
Transport, Storage and Post	4,217
Information Transmission, Computer Services and Software	2,881
Wholesale and Retail Trades	11,511
Hotels and Catering Services	772
Financial Intermediation	2,330
Real Estate	28,798
Leasing and Business Services	10,362
Scientific Research, Technical Service and Geologic Prospecting	2,750

Management of Water Conservancy, Environment and Public Facilities	1,036
Services to Households and Other Services	657
Education	18
Health, Social Security and Social Welfare	64
Culture, Sports and Entertainment	821
Public Management and Social Organizations	0

Foreign Investment by Form

	Million Dollars
Total	118,721
Foreign Direct Investments	117,586
Equity Joint Venture	23,772
Contractual Joint Venture	1,944
Wholly Foreign-owned Enterprise	89,589
FDI Shareholding Inc.	2,281
Joint Exploration	0
Others	0
Other Foreign Investment	1,134
Sale Share	326
International Lease	0
Compensation Trade	0
Processing and Assembly	808

China's Direct Investment Abroad by Country/Region

	Million Dollars
Total	107,844
Hong Kong, China	62,824

Cayman Islands	9,253
United States	3,873
Australia	3,458
Virgin Is. (E)	3,222
Singapore	2,033
Indonesia	1,563
United Kingdom	1,420
Russia	1,022
Canada	1,009
Germany	911
Thailand	755
Vietnam	481
Japan	434
Macao, China	395
Republic of Korea	269
France	260
Nigeria	209
Algeria	191
New Zealand	190
Sudan	141
Guinea	100
Mexico	50
Madagascar	16
South Africa	—

China's Direct Investment Abroad by Industry

	Million Dollars
Total	107,844
Leasing and Business Services	27,056
Mining	24,808
Financial Intermediation	15,105

Wholesale and Retail Trades	14,647
Manufacturing	7,197
Construction	4,364
Real Estate	3,953
Transport, Storage and Post	3,307
Agriculture, Forestry, Animal Husbandry and Fishery	1,813
Scientific Research and Technical Services	1,792
Information Transmission, Software and Information Technology	1,401
Service to Households, Repair and Other Services	1,129
Production and Supply of Electricity, Heat, Gas and Water	680
Culture, Sports and Entertainment	311
Management of Water Conservancy, Environment and Public Facilities	145
Hotels and Catering Services	82
Education	36
Health and Social Service	17
Public Management, Social Security and Social Organization	—

Research and Development

R&D Manpower (Full-time Equivalent)

	Thousand Man-years
Total	3,533
Basic Research	223
Applied Research	396
Experimental Development	2,914

R&D Expenditure

	Billion Yuan
Total	1,184.7
Basic Research	55.5
Applied Research	126.9
Experimental Development	1,002.3
Government Funds	250.1
Self-raised Funds by Enterprises	883.8
Ratio of Expenditure on R&D to GDP (%)	2.08

R&D Output

	Number
Scientific Papers Issued	1,544,550
Publication on Science and Technology	45,730
Major Achievements in Science and Technology	52,477
National Invention Prizes Awarded	71
National Scientific and Technological Progress Prizes Awarded	188
Patents Accepted	2,377,061
Inventions	825,136
Patents Granted	1,313,000
Inventions	207,688

Patents by International Classifications

	Application Accepted	Application Granted Number
Total	1,679,337	900,533
Personal Use Items	309,870	151,812
Industrial and Transportation	381,891	230,044
Chemistry and Metallurgy	154,289	70,019
Textiles and Papers Making	30,820	15,664
Fixed Construction	98,501	60,953
Mechanical Engineering	199,911	120,575
Physics	260,213	119,657
Electricity	243,842	131,809

Agriculture

Sown Area of Farm Crops

	Thousand Hectares
Total Sown Area	164,627
Grain Crops	111,956
Cereal	93,769
Rice	30,312
Wheat	24,117
Corn	36,318
Beans	9,224
Tubers	8,963
Oil-bearing Crops	14,023
Cottons	4,346
Fiber Crops	92
Sugar Crops	1,998
Tobacco	1,623
Vegetables	20,899
Area of Tea Plantations	2,469
Area of Orchards	12,371

Production of Principal Crops

	Thousand Tons
Grain	601,938
Cereal	552,692
Rice	203,612
Wheat	121,926
Corn	218,489
Beans	15,953
Tubers	33,293

Oil-bearing Crops	35,170
Peanuts	16,972
Rapeseeds	14,458
Sesame	623
Cottons	6,299
Fiber Crops	229
Jute and Ambary Hemp	61
Sugarcane	128,201
Beetroots	9,260
Tobacco	3,374
Flue-Cured Tobacco	3,149
Silkworm Cocoons	892
Mulberry Silkworm Cocoons	817
Tea	1,924
Fruits	250,930

Ave. Production of Principal Crops

	kg/hectare
Cereal	5,894
Cottons	1,449
Peanuts	3,663
Rapeseeds	1,920
Sesames	1,490
Jute and Ambary Hemp	3,581
Sugarcane	70,576
Beetroots	50,922
Flue-Cured Tobacco	2,062

Production of Livestock

	Thousand Tons
Output, of Meat	85,350
Pork, Beef and Muttons	65,744
Pork	54,930
Beef	6,732
Muttons	4,081
Milk	36,495
Cow Milk	35,314
Poultry Eggs	28,761
Total Aquatic Products	61,720
Seawater Aquatic Products	31,388
Freshwater Aquatic Products	30,332

Per Capita Output of Farm Products

	kg
Grain	443.5
Cottons	4.6
Oil-bearing Crops	25.9
Pork, Beef and Muttons	48.6
Total Aquatic Products	45.5
Milk	26.1

Industry

Number and Assets of Enterprises by Industry

	Number	Total Assets Billion Yuan
Total	352,546	85,063
Mining	17,481	8,698
Manufacturing	326,998	65,123
Production and Supply of Electricity, Gas and Water	8,067	11,242

Revenue and Profits of Enterprises by Industry

	Revenue	Total Profits Billion Yuan
Total	102,915	6,283
Mining	6,679	810
Manufacturing	90,194	5,071
Production and Supply of Electricity, Gas and Water	6,041	402

Number of Enterprises by Status of Registration

	Number
Domestic Funded	295,144
State-owned Enterprises	6,831
Collective-owned Enterprises	4,817
Cooperative Enterprises	2,384
Joint Ownership Enterprises	479
State Joint Ownership Enterprises	103
Collective Joint Ownership Enterprises	130

Joint State-collective Enterprises	101
Other Joint Ownership Enterprises	145
Limited Liability Corporations	69,439
State Sole Funded Corporations	1,478
Other Limited Liability Corporations	67,961
Share-holding Corporations Limited	9,077
Private Enterprises	194,945
Private-funded Enterprises	35,002
Private Partnership Enterprises	5,623
Private Limited Liability Corporations	147,023
Private Share-holding Corporations Ltd.	7,297
Other Enterprises	7,172
Enterprises with Funds from Hong Kong, Macao and Taiwan	26,202
Joint-venture Enterprises	8,544
Cooperative Enterprises	818
Enterprises with Sole Investment	16,298
Share-holding Corporations Ltd.	478
Other Enterprises with Funds from Hong Kong, Macao and Taiwan	64
Foreign Funded Enterprises	31,200
Joint-venture Enterprises	11,585
Cooperation Enterprises	865
Enterprises with Sole Funds	18,109
Share-holding Corporations Ltd.	513
Other Foreign Funded Enterprises	128

Assets of Enterprises by Status of Registration

	Billion Yuan
Domestic Funded	66,501.5
State-owned Enterprises	11,000.2

Collective-owned Enterprises	617.3
Cooperative Enterprises	329.2
Joint Ownership Enterprises	111.3
State Joint Ownership Enterprises	64.6
Collective Joint Ownership Enterprises	10.6
Joint State-collective Enterprises	21.2
Other Joint Ownership Enterprises	14.8
Limited Liability Corporations	25,443.0
State Sole Funded Corporations	5,423.4
Other Limited Liability Corporations	20,019.7
Share-holding Corporations Limited	10,615.9
Private Enterprises	17,477.1
Private-funded Enterprises	2,040.2
Private Partnership Enterprises	302.9
Private Limited Liability Corporations	13,697.1
Private Share-holding Corporations Ltd.	1,436.9
Other Enterprises	907.4
Enterprises with Funds from Hong Kong, Macao and Taiwan	7,181.5
Joint-venture Enterprises	2,725.3
Cooperative Enterprises	159.4
Enterprises with Sole Investment	3,840.7
Share-holding Corporations Ltd.	436.9
Other Enterprises with Funds from Hong Kong, Macao and Taiwan	19.2
Foreign Funded Enterprises	11,379.6
Joint-venture Enterprises	5,270.7
Cooperation Enterprises	293.4
Enterprises with Sole Funds	5,193.5
Share-holding Corporations Ltd.	592.3
Other Foreign Funded Enterprises	29.7

Revenue from Principal Business of Enterprises by Status of Registration

	Billion Yuan
Domestic Funded	78,776.2
State-owned Enterprises	8,258.0
Collective-owned Enterprises	1,151.4
Cooperative Enterprises	439.1
Joint Ownership Enterprises	120.1
State Joint Ownership Enterprises	55.3
Collective Joint Ownership Enterprises	23.6
Joint State-collective Enterprises	17.2
Other Joint Ownership Enterprises	24.0
Limited Liability Corporations	24,883.9
State Sole Funded Corporations	3,387.5
Other Limited Liability Corporations	21,496.4
Share-holding Corporations Limited	9,414.4
Private Enterprises	32,969.4
Private-funded Enterprises	5,477.5
Private Partnership Enterprises	750.6
Private Limited Liability Corporations	24,656.2
Private Share-holding Corporations Ltd.	2,085.2
Other Enterprises	1,539.9
Enterprises with Funds from Hong Kong, Macao and Taiwan	8,801.6
Joint-venture Enterprises	3,021.2
Cooperative Enterprises	213.0
Enterprises with Sole Investment	5,151.9
Share-holding Corporations Ltd.	391.5
Other Enterprises with Funds from Hong Kong, Macao and Taiwan	24.1
Foreign Funded Enterprises	15,337.1
Joint-venture Enterprises	7,076.7

Cooperation Enterprises	315.7
Enterprises with Sole Funds	7,374.0
Share-holding Corporations Ltd.	523.3
Other Foreign Funded Enterprises	47.4

Profits of Enterprises by Status of Registration

	Billion Yuan
Domestic Funded	4,823.2
State-owned Enterprises	403.1
Collective-owned Enterprises	82.5
Cooperative Enterprises	27.5
Joint Ownership Enterprises	6.5
State Joint Ownership Enterprises	2.3
Collective Joint Ownership Enterprises	1.3
Joint State-collective Enterprises	1.2
Other Joint Ownership Enterprises	1.7
Limited Liability Corporations	1,374.1
State Sole Funded Corporations	144.1
Other Limited Liability Corporations	1,230.0
Share-holding Corporations Ltd.	743.5
Private Enterprises	2,087.6
Private-funded Enterprises	420.0
Private Partnership Enterprises	56.7
Private Limited Liability Corporations	1,475.3
Private Share-holding Corporations Ltd.	135.6
Other Enterprises	98.4
Enterprises with Funds from Hong Kong, Macao and Taiwan	492.6
Joint-venture Enterprises	176.6
Cooperative Enterprises	17.3

Enterprises with Sole Investment	271.8
Share-holding Corporations Ltd.	26.0
Other Enterprises with Funds from Hong Kong, Macao and Taiwan	0.9
Foreign Funded Enterprises	967.3
Joint-venture Enterprises	527.3
Cooperation Enterprises	21.5
Enterprises with Sole Funds	373.4
Share-holding Corporations Ltd.	41.8
Other Foreign Funded Enterprises	3.3

Real Estate

Number of Real Estate Enterprises

	Number
Total	91,444
Domestic Funded	86,379
State-owned Enterprises	1,739
Collective-owned Enterprises	570
Enterprises with Funds from Hong Kong, Macao and Taiwan	3,391
Foreign Funded	1,674

Main Indicators on Real Estate Development

	2013
Land Space Purchased This Year ('000 sq. m)	388,144
Investment Completed This Year (¥ billion)	8,601
Total Actual Funds in Place This Year (¥ billion)	12,212
Floor Space of Buildings ('000 sq. m)	
Floor Space under Construction	66,557
Floor Space Completed	10,143
Floor Space Started This Year	20,121
Residential Buildings	14,584
Floor Space of Commercialized Buildings Sold ('000 sq. m)	13,055
Residential Buildings	11,572
Average Selling Price of Commercialized Buildings (¥/sq. m)	6,237
Residential Buildings	5,850

Construction

Number of Construction Enterprises

	Number
Total	79,528
State-owned	4,607
Collective-owned	4,572
Funded from Hong Kong, Macao and Taiwan	389
Foreign Funded	280
Others	69,680

Gross Output Value of Construction Enterprises

	Billion Yuan
Total	15,931.2
State-owned	2,616.1
Collective-owned	554.3
Funded from Hong Kong, Macao and Taiwan	66.1
Foreign Funded	60.3
Others	12,634.4

Wholesale and Retail Trade

Number of Corporation Enterprises

	Number
Total	171,973
Wholesale Trade	91,607
Retail Trade	80,366

Total Purchases Value

	Billion Yuan
Total	45,126.6
Wholesale Trade	36,525.1
Retail Trade	8,601.5

Hotels and Catering Services

Corporation Enterprises

	Number
Total	45,180
Hotels	18,437
Catering Services	26,743

Business Revenue

	Billion Yuan
Total	806.1
Hotels	352.8
Catering Services	453.3

External Trade

Total Value of Imports and Exports of Goods

	Million Dollars
Total Imports and Exports	4,158,993
Total Exports	2,209,004
Primary Goods	107,268
Manufactured Goods	2,101,736
Total Imports	1,949,989
Primary Goods	658,081
Manufactured Goods	1,291,909
Balance	259,015

Exports Value by Category of Goods

	Million Dollars
Total	2,209,004
A Primary Goods	107,268
Food and Live Animals Used Mainly for Food	55,726
Beverages and Tobacco	2,609
Non-edible Raw Materials	14,563
Mineral Fuels, Lubricants and Related Materials	33,786
Animal and Vegetable Oils, Fats and Wax	584
B Manufactured Goods	2,101,736
Chemicals and Related Products	119,618
Light Textile Industrial Products, Rubber Products, Minerals and Metallurgical Products	360,606
Machinery and Transport Equipment	1,038,534
Miscellaneous Products	581,249
Other Products	1,729

Imports Value by Category of Goods

	Million Dollars
Total	1,949,989
A Primary Goods	658,081
Food and Live Animals Used Mainly for Food	41,701
Beverages and Tobacco	4,509
Non-edible Raw Materials	286,371
Mineral Fuels, Lubricants and Related Materials	315,160
Animal and Vegetable Oils, Fats and Wax	10,339
B Manufactured Goods	1,291,909
Chemicals and Related Products	190,304
Light Textile Industrial Products, Rubber Products, Minerals and Metallurgical Products	147,872
Machinery and Transport Equipment	710,141
Miscellaneous Products	138,855
Other Products	104,736

Value of Imports and Exports by Country (Region) of Origin/Destination

		Million Dollars
	Total	4,158,993
1	**Asia**	2,224,008
2	**Europe**	729,916
3	**North America**	575,467
4	United States	520,749
5	Hong Kong, China	400,701
6	Japan	312,378
7	Korea Rep.	274,238

8	**Latin America**	261,390
9	**Africa**	210,254
10	Taiwan, China	197,039
11	Germany	161,498
12	P. R. China	157,540
13	**Oceanic and Pacific Islands**	153,309
14	Australia	136,508
15	Malaysia	106,083
16	Brazil	90,195
17	Russia	89,259
18	Singapore	75,896
19	Saudi Arabia	72,191
20	Thailand	71,241
21	Netherlands	70,140
22	United Kingdom	70,021
23	Indonesia	68,355
24	Vietnam	65,478
25	India	65,403
26	South Africa	65,219
27	Switzerland	59,588
28	Canada	54,454
29	France	49,824
30	United Arab Emirates	46,235
31	Italy	43,326
32	Iran	39,427
33	Mexico	39,205
34	Philippines	38,050
35	Angola	35,937
36	Chile	33,813
37	Kazakhstan	28,596
38	Belgium	25,408
39	Spain	24,900

40	Iraq	24,879
41	Oman	22,941
42	Turkey	22,233
43	Venezuela	19,185
44	Argentina	14,836
45	Poland	14,807
46	Peru	14,597
47	Pakistan	14,216
48	Sweden	13,786
49	Nigeria	13,589
50	New Zealand	12,385
51	Kuwait	12,262
52	Ukraine	11,122
53	Panama	11,037
54	Israel	10,827
55	Colombia	10,446
56	Bangladesh	10,307
57	Egypt	10,214
58	Myanmar	10,196
59	Qatar	10,174
60	Turkmenistan	10,031
61	Finland	9,737
62	Czech	9,453
63	Denmark	9,087
64	Hungary	8,407
65	Algeria	8,188
66	Austria	7,068
67	Ireland	6,670
68	Korea DPR	6,558
69	Slovak	6,543
70	Congo	6,491
71	Norway	6,205

72	Mongolia	5,959
73	Costa Rica	5,685
74	Republic of Yemen	5,200
75	Ghana	5,149
76	Kirghizia	5,138
77	Libya	4,874
78	Uruguay	4,790
79	**Others**	4,650
80	Uzbekistan	4,551
81	Sudan	4,498
82	Romania	4,030
83	Portugal	3,906
84	Morocco	3,803
85	Zambia	3,778
86	Cambodia	3,773
87	Ecuador	3,742
88	Congo DR	3,694
89	Tanzania	3,693
90	Greece	3,652
91	Sri Lanka	3,619
92	Jordan	3,604
93	Macao, China	3,558
94	Kenya	3,270
95	Malta	3,240
96	Benin	3,198
97	Eq. Guinea	2,827
98	Laos	2,733
99	Togo	2,561
100	Republic of South Sudan	2,543
101	Lebanon	2,536
102	Liberia	2,500
103	Mauritania	2,327

104	Nepal	2,254
105	Ethiopia	2,184
106	Slovenia	2,136
107	Bulgaria	2,074
108	Luxembourg	2,064
109	Tadzhikistan	1,958
110	Cameroon	1,881
111	Cuba	1,879
112	Lithuania	1,811
113	Brunei	1,794
114	Puerto Rico	1,710
115	Mozambique	1,654
116	Guatemala	1,649
117	Sierra Leone	1,605
118	Bahrain	1,544
119	Marshall Is.	1,500
120	Croatia	1,494
121	Latvia	1,473
122	Byelorussia	1,453
123	Tunisia	1,440
124	Paraguay	1,417
125	Papua New Guinea	1,351
126	Dominica Rep.	1,336
127	Gabon	1,331
128	Estonia	1,309
129	Cote d'Ivoire	1,213
130	Azerbaijan	1,102
131	Zimbabwe	1,102
132	Senegal	1,037
133	Honduras	1,034
134	Cyprus	1,025
135	Djibouti	1,019

136	Guinea	992
137	Georgia	917
138	Madagascar	817
139	Bolivia	807
140	Namibia	740
141	Syria	695
142	Mauritius	662
143	Jamaica	631
144	Nicaragua	615
145	Serbia	612
146	Albania	559
147	El Salvador	531
148	Uganda	524
149	Chad	475
150	Solomon Is.	441
151	Trinidad and Tobago	441
152	Mali	427
153	Gambia	386
154	Vanuatu	383
155	Botswana	342
156	Haiti	339
157	Afghanistan	338
158	Bahamas	337
159	Fiji	304
160	Burkina Faso	290
161	Malawi	252
162	Antigua and Barbuda	246
163	Rwanda	243
164	Iceland	222
165	New Caledonia (Fr)	220
166	Surinam	202
167	Niger	200

168	Armenia	193
169	Bermuda	190
170	Eritrea	189
171	Guyana	181
172	Macedonia	171
173	Somalia	150
174	Swaziland	140
175	Reunion	134
176	Liechtenstein	133
177	Moldavia	131
178	Belize	131
179	Bosnia and Herzegovina	112
180	Lesotho	103
181	Montenegro	103
182	Maldives	98
183	Palestine	91
184	Barbados	83
185	Mayotte	78
186	Faroe Islands	76
187	Greenland	72
188	Cape Verde	62
189	Burundi	60
190	Andreas Is. (N)	60
191	Samoa	54
192	Central Africa	50
193	Polynesia (F)	49
194	Timor Leste	48
195	Gibraltar	48
196	Seychelles	39
197	Tonsga	39
198	Monaco	38
199	Guadeloupe	31

200	Comoros	30
201	Guinea-Bissau	29
202	Saint Vincent and Grenadines	25
203	Martinique	24
204	Dominica	23
205	Curacao	22
206	Aruba	21
207	Cook Is.	20
208	Saint Lucia	20
209	Kiribati	19
210	Bhutan	17
211	St. Kitts-Nevis	16
212	Micronesia Commonwealth	15
213	French Guyana	15
214	Cayman Is.	11
215	Virgin Is. (E)	11
216	Granada	8
217	Melilla	8
218	Tuvalu	8
219	Sao Tome and Principe	5
220	Society Is.	4
221	San Marino	4
222	Canary Is.	3
223	Republic of Palau	3
224	Saint Martin Is.	3
225	Other Countries (Regions) in Latin America	3
226	Andorra	2
227	Other Countries (Regions) in Latin America	2
228	Other Countries (Regions) in Latin America	1

229	Saba	1
230	Nauru	1
231	Wallis and Futuna	1
232	Ceuta	1
233	Norfolk Islands	1

Value of Exports by Country (Region) of Origin/Destination

		Million Dollars
	Total	2,209,004
1	**Asia**	1,134,070
2	**Europe**	405,744
3	**North America**	397,815
4	Hong Kong, China	384,495
5	United States	368,406
6	Japan	150,132
7	**Latin America**	133,961
8	**Africa**	92,799
9	Korea Rep.	91,165
10	Germany	67,343
11	Netherlands	60,315
12	United Kingdom	50,942
13	Russia	49,591
14	Vietnam	48,586
15	India	48,432
16	Malaysia	45,931
17	Singapore	45,832
18	**Oceanic and Pacific Islands**	44,615
19	Taiwan, China	40,634
20	Australia	37,554
21	Indonesia	36,930
22	Brazil	35,895

23	United Arab Emirates	33,411
24	Thailand	32,718
25	Canada	29,217
26	Mexico	28,966
27	France	26,714
28	Italy	25,753
29	Philippines	19,868
30	Spain	18,928
31	Saudi Arabia	18,740
32	Turkey	17,747
33	South Africa	16,831
34	Belgium	15,560
35	Iran	14,037
36	Chile	13,105
37	Poland	12,575
38	Kazakhstan	12,545
39	Nigeria	12,043
40	Pakistan	11,020
41	Panama	10,993
42	Bangladesh	9,705
43	Argentina	8,750
44	Egypt	8,363
45	Ukraine	7,849
46	Israel	7,645
47	Myanmar	7,339
48	Iraq	6,894
49	Czech	6,838
50	Colombia	6,826
51	Sweden	6,799
52	Peru	6,189
53	Venezuela	6,065
54	Algeria	6,024
55	Finland	5,832

56	Denmark	5,711
57	Hungary	5,692
58	Kirghizia	5,075
59	New Zealand	4,132
60	Angola	3,964
61	Ghana	3,946
62	Korea DPR	3,630
63	Switzerland	3,511
64	Sri Lanka	3,437
65	Jordan	3,435
66	Cambodia	3,410
67	Morocco	3,272
68	Greece	3,219
69	Kenya	3,217
70	Macao, China	3,171
71	Tanzania	3,141
72	Slovak	3,084
73	Benin	2,992
74	Ecuador	2,967
75	Libya	2,835
76	Romania	2,823
77	Norway	2,737
78	Kuwait	2,676
79	Uzbekistan	2,613
80	Malta	2,515
81	Portugal	2,507
82	Lebanon	2,491
83	Ireland	2,477
84	Mongolia	2,450
85	Togo	2,443
86	Sudan	2,398
87	Liberia	2,336
88	Uruguay	2,324

89	Nepal	2,211
90	Republic of Yemen	2,139
91	Austria	2,038
92	Oman	1,901
93	Tadzhikistan	1,869
94	Ethiopia	1,868
95	Slovenia	1,833
96	Luxembourg	1,808
97	Laos	1,723
98	Qatar	1,711
99	Brunei	1,704
100	Lithuania	1,686
101	Cameroon	1,515
102	Guatemala	1,475
103	Marshall Is.	1,422
104	Croatia	1,390
105	Cuba	1,375
106	Latvia	1,374
107	Paraguay	1,357
108	Tunisia	1,263
109	Bahrain	1,239
110	Mozambique	1,199
111	Turkmenistan	1,138
112	Bulgaria	1,117
113	Estonia	1,110
114	Dominica Rep.	1,046
115	Djibouti	1,019
116	Senegal	997
117	Cyprus	972
118	Cote d'Ivoire	956
119	Congo DR	949
120	Costa Rica	927
121	Guinea	907

122	Byelorussia	872
123	Azerbaijan	869
124	Georgia	862
125	Honduras	799
126	Congo	779
127	Zambia	730
128	Syria	690
129	Puerto Rico	657
130	Mauritius	649
131	Madagascar	643
132	Jamaica	627
133	Mauritania	598
134	Papua New Guinea	553
135	Bolivia	531
136	Nicaragua	523
137	El Salvador	522
138	Namibia	482
139	Uganda	452
140	Gabon	433
141	Serbia	432
142	Zimbabwe	414
143	Vanuatu	380
144	Chad	372
145	Eq. Guinea	358
146	Bahamas	337
147	Afghanistan	328
148	Albania	325
149	Haiti	323
150	Trinidad and Tobago	321
151	Gambia	309
152	Mali	275
153	Antigua and Barbuda	245
154	Fiji	244

155	Malawi	214
156	Bermuda	190
157	Niger	184
158	Surinam	174
159	Guyana	160
160	Sierra Leone	153
161	Botswana	148
162	Iceland	147
163	Eritrea	138
164	Rwanda	134
165	Reunion	134
166	Somalia	134
167	Belize	122
168	Armenia	120
169	Moldavia	113
170	Burkina Faso	103
171	Maldives	97
172	Bosnia and Herzegovina	91
173	Palestine	91
174	New Caledonia (Fr)	90
175	Lesotho	90
176	Montenegro	86
177	Mayotte	78
178	Republic of South Sudan	75
179	Barbados	70
180	Macedonia	63
181	Cape Verde	62
182	Andreas Is. (N)	60
183	Samoa	54
184	Burundi	51
185	Timor Leste	47
186	Polynesia (F)	45
187	Gibraltar	42

188	Seychelles	39
189	Tonga	38
190	Solomon Is.	37
191	Guadeloupe	30
192	Comoros	30
193	Monaco	29
194	Saint Vincent and Grenadines	25
195	Swaziland	25
196	Martinique	24
197	Dominica	23
198	Aruba	21
199	Curacao	20
200	Saint Lucia	20
201	Cook Is.	19
202	Kiribati	19
203	Liechtenstein	18
204	Bhutan	17
205	St. Kitts-Nevis	16
206	French Guyana	15
207	Guinea-Bissau	12
208	Cayman Is.	11
209	Virgin Is. (E)	11
210	Central Africa	9
211	Granada	8
212	Melilla	8
213	Tuvalu	8
214	Micronesia Commonwealth	5
215	Sao Tome and Principe	5
216	Society Is.	4
217	Republic of Palau	3
218	Canary Is.	3
219	Saint Martin Is.	3

220	Other Countries (Regions) in Latin America	3
221	Andorra	2
222	San Marino	2
223	Other Countries (Regions) in Latin America	2
224	Faroe Islands	1
225	Saba	1
226	Nauru	1
227	Wallis and Futuna	1
228	Ceuta	1
229	Other Countries (Regions) in Latin America	1
230	Norfolk Islands	1

Value of Imports by Country (Region) of Origin/Destination

		Million Dollars
	Total	1,949,989
1	**Asia**	1,089,938
2	**Europe**	324,172
3	Korea Rep.	183,073
4	**North America**	177,651
5	Japan	162,245
6	P. R. China	157,540
7	Taiwan, China	156,405
8	United States	152,342
9	**Latin America**	127,429
10	**Africa**	117,455
11	**Oceanic and Pacific Islands**	108,694
12	Australia	98,954
13	Germany	94,156

14	Malaysia	60,153
15	Switzerland	56,076
16	Brazil	54,299
17	Saudi Arabia	53,451
18	South Africa	48,388
19	Russia	39,668
20	Thailand	38,523
21	Angola	31,973
22	Indonesia	31,424
23	Singapore	30,065
24	Iran	25,390
25	Canada	25,237
26	France	23,110
27	Oman	21,041
28	Chile	20,708
29	United Kingdom	19,079
30	Philippines	18,182
31	Iraq	17,985
32	Italy	17,574
33	India	16,970
34	Vietnam	16,892
35	Hong Kong, China	16,207
36	Kazakhstan	16,051
37	Venezuela	13,120
38	United Arab Emirates	12,824
39	Mexico	10,238
40	Belgium	9,848
41	Netherlands	9,825
42	Kuwait	9,587
43	Turkmenistan	8,893
44	Qatar	8,463
45	Peru	8,408
46	New Zealand	8,253

47	Sweden	6,987
48	Argentina	6,086
49	Spain	5,972
50	Congo	5,712
51	Austria	5,030
52	Costa Rica	4,758
53	**Others**	4,650
54	Turkey	4,486
55	Ireland	4,193
56	Finland	3,906
57	Colombia	3,620
58	Mongolia	3,510
59	Norway	3,468
60	Slovak	3,458
61	Denmark	3,376
62	Ukraine	3,273
63	Pakistan	3,197
64	Israel	3,181
65	Republic of Yemen	3,061
66	Zambia	3,048
67	Korea DPR	2,927
68	Myanmar	2,857
69	Congo DR	2,746
70	Hungary	2,715
71	Czech	2,615
72	Eq. Guinea	2,470
73	Republic of South Sudan	2,468
74	Uruguay	2,466
75	Poland	2,232
76	Algeria	2,165
77	Sudan	2,100
78	Libya	2,039

79	Uzbekistan	1,938
80	Egypt	1,852
81	Mauritania	1,729
82	Nigeria	1,547
83	Sierra Leone	1,453
84	Portugal	1,399
85	Romania	1,208
86	Ghana	1,203
87	Puerto Rico	1,052
88	Laos	1,010
89	Bulgaria	957
90	Gabon	899
91	Papua New Guinea	798
92	Ecuador	775
93	Malta	725
94	Zimbabwe	688
95	Bangladesh	602
96	Byelorussia	581
97	Tanzania	553
98	Morocco	531
99	Cuba	505
100	Mozambique	455
101	Greece	433
102	Solomon Is.	405
103	Macao, China	387
104	Cameroon	366
105	Cambodia	364
106	Ethiopia	316
107	Bahrain	305
108	Slovenia	303
109	Dominica Rep.	290
110	Bolivia	276

111	Namibia	258
112	Cote d'Ivoire	257
113	Luxembourg	257
114	Honduras	235
115	Albania	235
116	Azerbaijan	234
117	Benin	206
118	Estonia	200
119	Botswana	194
120	Burkina Faso	187
121	Sri Lanka	183
122	Serbia	180
123	Tunisia	177
124	Guatemala	174
125	Madagascar	174
126	Jordan	170
127	Liberia	164
128	Mali	152
129	New Caledonia (Fr)	129
130	Lithuania	125
131	Trinidad and Tobago	120
132	Togo	118
133	Liechtenstein	115
134	Swaziland	115
135	Rwanda	108
136	Macedonia	108
137	Croatia	104
138	Chad	104
139	Latvia	99
140	Nicaragua	92
141	Brunei	90
142	Tadzhikistan	89

143	Guinea	84
144	Gambia	78
145	Marshall Is.	78
146	Iceland	76
147	Faroe Islands	75
148	Armenia	73
149	Greenland	72
150	Uganda	72
151	Kirghizia	62
152	Paraguay	61
153	Fiji	59
154	Georgia	54
155	Cyprus	53
156	Kenya	53
157	Eritrea	51
158	Lebanon	46
159	Panama	44
160	Nepal	43
161	Central Africa	41
162	Senegal	40
163	Malawi	38
164	Surinam	28
165	Guyana	21
166	Bosnia and Herzegovina	21
167	Moldavia	19
168	Guinea-Bissau	17
169	Somalia	16
170	Montenegro	16
171	Niger	16
172	Haiti	15
173	Lesotho	13
174	Mauritius	13

175	Barbados	13
176	Micronesia Commonwealth	10
177	Afghanistan	10
178	Burundi	9
179	El Salvador	9
180	Monaco	9
181	Belize	8
182	Gibraltar	6
183	Syria	5
184	Polynesia (F)	4
185	Jamaica	4
186	Vanuatu	2
187	San Marino	2
188	Curacao	1
189	Cook Is.	1
190	Other Countries (Regions) in Latin America	1

Main Exported Goods in Value

	Million Dollars
Live Hogs	459.2
Live Poultry	29.8
Frozen, Fresh Beef	44.3
Frozen, Fresh Pork	325.4
Frozen Chicken	242.1
Aquatic and Seawater Products	19,429.2
Fresh Eggs	106.9
Cereals and Cereals Flour	664.2
Rice	416.7
Maize	33.2
Vegetables	9,005.5
Fresh Vegetables	3,401.7

Mandarins and Oranges	991.2
Apples	1,029.9
Pine Nut Kernels	212.3
Soybean	201.9
Peanuts	219.1
Edible Vegetable Oil	193.1
Sugar	41.8
Natural Honey	246.6
Tea	1,246.3
Dried Capsicum	109.9
Canned Pork	149.4
Canned Mushroom	527.2
Beer	162.9
Casings	961.6
Feathers and Down for Stuffing	1,002.3
Medical Materials and Medicaments of Chinese Type	1,198.0
Flue-cured Tobacco	457.8
Cigarette	488.9
Wood Sawn	324.0
Raw Silk	373.6
Cashmere	285.9
Cottons (Cottons Wool)	15.2
Natural Graphite	276.6
Natural Magnesium Carbonate, Magnesia	529.4
Fluorite	137.6
Barite	279.5
Talcum	166.7
Aluminum Oxide	95.1
Coal and Lignite	1,061.9
Coke and Semi-coke	1,134.1
Crude Oil	1,456.2
Petroleum Products Refined	24,505.0

Paraffin Wax	630.4
Tungstate	90.8
Zinc Oxide and Zinc Peroxide	17.3
Synthetic Organic Dyestuffs	1,490.4
Medical and Pharmaceutical Products	12,320.4
Medicaments of Chinese Type	268.7
Pharmaceutical Goods	1,353.0
Detergent	328.0
Fireworks and Firecrackers	771.3
Resin and Resin Acids	272.2
Rubber Tyres	16,152.9
Paper and Paperboard in Rolls	6,812.9
Cottons Yarn	2,515.2
Silk	964.6
Cottons Cloth	15,508.1
Flax or Ramie Woven Fabric	946.6
Synthetic Short Fiber and Cottons-fiber Mixture Woven Fabric	2,723.4
Carpets	2,505.5
Bags of PP or PE Strip (Except Turnover Bags)	1,074.8
Cement and Cement Clinkers	795.7
Plate Glass	1,043.5
Glass Products	7,960.2
Porcelain and Pottery Ware for Household Use	4,702.0
Pig Iron and Spiegeleisen	110.4
Billet and Crude Forgings	3.7
Rolled Steel	53,212.5
Unwrought Copper and Its Alloys	2,266.4
Rolled Copper	4,176.5
Unwrought Aluminum and Its Alloys	1,280.0
Rolled Aluminum	10,405.8

Unwrought Zinc and Zinc Alloys	12.3
Unwrought Tin and Tin Alloys	70.3
Unwrought Antimony	21.2
Unwrought Manganese	487.0
Iron or Copper Nails, Bolts, etc.	4,709.4
Hand Tools and Tools for Machines	8,681.1
Fans	4,165.6
Textile Machinery	2,513.9
Sewing Machines	1,375.9
Machine Tools	2,858.5
Electric Calculator	660.6
Automatic Data Processing Machines and Components	182,169.2
Parts for Auto Data Processing Equipment	28,598.9
Bearings	3,390.0
Electric Motors and Generators	9,862.5
Static Converters	17,613.6
Primary Cells and Batteries	1,943.9
Electric Accumulators	7,591.6
Telephone Sets	97,152.6
Radio Sets (including Sound Recording Apparatus)	4,466.8
TV Sets (including a Complete Set of Spare Parts)	11,053.3
Electrical Capacitors	7,326.8
Electrical Apparatus for Switching or Protecting Electrical Circuits	21,614.1
Diode and Semi-Conductors	25,058.8
Insulated Wire or Cable	18,396.9
Containers	7,880.5
Motor Vehicles (including a Complete Set of Spare Parts)	11,975.2
Parts of Motor Vehicles	29,055.6

Bicycles	3,169.2
Ships	25,927.1
Cameras	4,694.9
Medical Instruments and Appliances	8,180.2
Wrist Watches	2,200.1
Clocks	1,083.3
Furniture	51,822.8
Garments (Excluding Knitwear and Crochet)	61,002.1
Garments, Knitted or Crocheted	86,892.8
Leather Shoes	12,010.7
Cloth Shoes with Outer of Rubber or Artificial Plastic Materials	9,629.6
Plastic Articles	35,293.2
Toys	12,378.9
Footballs, Basketballs and Volleyballs	539.6
Umbrellas	2,689.0
Bamboo Products	177.9
Rattan Products	93.1
Straw Mats and Straw Products	136.0
Wickerwork	429.4
Mechanical and Electrical Products	1,264,662.5
High and New-tech Products	660,081.3

Main Imported Goods in Value

	Million Dollars
Cereals and Cereals Flour	5,100.6
Wheat	1,880.6
Paddy and Rice	1,083.0
Soybean	38,009.4
Edible Vegetable Oil	8,074.9
Sugar	2,068.7

Natural Rubber (including Latex)	6,392.6
Synthetic Rubber (including Latex)	4,428.4
Logs	9,320.1
Wood Sawn	6,826.3
Paper Pulp	11,375.3
Wool and Wool Tops	2,839.8
Cottons	8,441.3
Synthetic Fibers Suitable for Spinning	1,154.4
Polyester Fibers	241.6
Polyacryolnitr Fibers	667.7
Iron Ore	106,175.4
Manganese Ores	3,192.4
Copper Ores	19,509.0
Chromium Ores	2,388.4
Aluminum Oxide	1,404.5
Coal and Lignite	29,066.4
Crude Oil	219,660.4
Petroleum Products Refined	32,025.7
Ethylene Glycol	8,679.6
Telephthalic Acid	2,988.3
Caprolactam	1,075.9
Pharmaceutical Products	16,216.2
Chemical Fertilizers, Manufactured (Actual Weight)	3,392.7
Urea	10.9
Compound Fertilizers of Nitrogen, Phosphor and Kalium	753.3
Diammonium Phosphape ('000 tons)	113.4
Potassium Chloride	2,376.6
Polyethylene in Primary Forms	9,582.7
Polypropylene in Primary Forms	5,595.9
Polystyrene in Primary Forms	6,407.9
ABS Copolymers	3,597.1

Polyvinyl Chloride in Primary Forms	1,226.1
Slices or Chips of Polyethylene Terephthalate	351.5
Pesticides	692.9
Paper and Paperboard (Un-chopped in Shape)	3,660.3
Rolled Steel	17,052.5
Copper and Copper Alloys	28,546.9
Rolled Copper	6,446.1
Aluminum and Aluminum Alloys	1,010.0
Rolled Aluminum	3,026.3
Boilers	42.9
Compressors for Refrigerating Equipment	1,149.8
Machine Tools	10,065.9
Valves	6,500.6
Automatic Data Processing Machines and Components	30,824.3
Telephone Sets	1,809.9
Sound Recording Apparatus (including a Complete Set of Spare Parts)	266.6
TV Sets	30.9
Cathode-ray TV Picture Tube	7.6
Motor Vehicles (including a Complete Set of Spare Parts)	48,716.8
Cars	17,618.3
Trucks	839.8
Dump Trucks	145.1
Chassis with Engines	135.8
Parts of Motor Vehicles	25,392.0
Aircraft	20,904.0
Ships	864.5
Medical Instruments and Appliances	7,892.8
Mechanical and Electrical Products	839,699.6
High and New-tech Products	557,942.2

Total Value of Imports and Exports of Services

	Million Dollars
Imports and Exports	539,645
Exports	210,594
Imports	329,051
Balance	−118,457

Total Value of Exports of Services by Sector

	Million Dollars
Total	210,594
Transportation	37,646
Travel	51,664
Communication Services	1,666
Construction Services	10,663
Insurance Services	3,996
Financial Services	2,915
Computer and Information Services	15,433
Royalties and License Fees	887
Consulting	40,536
Advertising, Media	4,906
Film, Audiovisual	147
Other Business Services	40,136

Total Value of Imports of Services by Sector

	Million Dollars
Total	329,051
Transportation	94,324
Travel	128,580
Communication Services	1,639

Construction Services	3,890
Insurance Services	22,093
Financial Services	3,416
Computer and Information Services	5,985
Royalties and License Fees	21,033
Consulting	23,584
Advertising, Media	3,134
Film, Audiovisual	783
Other Business Services	20,590

Transport and Communications

Length of Transport Routes

	Thousand Km
Railways in Operation	103
Highways	4,356
Expressway	104
Navigable Inland Waterways	126
Regular Civil Aviation Routes	4,106
Petroleum and Gas Pipelines	98

Total Passenger Traffic

	Thousand	Million Passenger-km
Total	21,229,915	2,757,165
Railways	2,105,969	1,059,562
Highways	18,534,630	1,125,094
Waterways	235,350	6,833
Civil Aviation	353,966	565,676

Cargo Handled

	Thousand Tons	Million Tons-km
Total	40,989,000	16,801,380
Railways	3,966,970	2,917,389
Highways	30,766,480	5,573,808
Waterways	5,597,850	7,943,565
Civil Aviation	5,613	17,029
Petroleum and Gas Pipelines	652,088	349,589

Motor Vehicle Population

	Number
Civil Motor Vehicles ('000)	126,701
Private Vehicles	105,017
Other Motor Vehicles ('000)	105,467
Civil Transport Vessels	**172,554**
Motor Vessels	155,340
Barges	17,214

Volume of Cargo Handled in Coastal Ports

	Thousand Tons
Total	7,280,980
Coal and Its Products	1,504,010
Petroleum, Natural Gas and Their Products	642,980
Metal Ores	1,243,280
Steel and Iron	258,480
Mineral Building Materials	529,350
Cement	55,130
Timber	51,110
Non-metal Ores	116,970
Chemical Fertilizers and Pesticides	23,360
Salt	9,050
Grain	158,350
Others	2,688,910

Business Volume of Postal Services

Number of Letters (million pcs)	6,341
Package ('000 pcs)	69
Pieces of Express Mail Services (10,000 pcs)	9,187

Issue of Newspapers and Magazines (10,000 copies)	151
Postal Remittance Transactions (10,000 times)	185
Commemorative and Special Stamps (10,000 pcs)	1,183
Number of Offices	125,115
Average Area Served by Every Postal Office (sq. km)	77

Business Volume of Telecommunication Services

Length of Local Calls of Fixed Telephone (million minutes)	302,309
Length of Long-distance Calls of Fixed Telephone (million minutes)	59,055
Length of Calls of Mobile Telephone (million minutes)	5,822,967
Short Message Services (million messages)	892,102
Number of Internet Users ('000)	617,580
Number of Mobile Telephone Subscribers at Year-end ('000 subscribers)	1,229,113
3G Mobile Phone Subscribers	401,611
Countries (regions) with Mobile Phone Roaming	258
Number of Fixed Telephone Subscribers at Year-end ('000 subscribers)	266,985
Urban Fixed Telephone Subscribers	184,568
Household Fixed Telephone Subscribers	104,743
Rural Fixed Telephone Subscribers	82,417
Household Fixed Telephone Subscribers	66,434
Public Telephone Subscribers	22,334

Capacity of Long Distance Telephone Exchanges ('000 lines)	12,805
Capacity of Office Telephone Exchanges ('000 lines)	410,893
Capacity of Mobile Telephone Exchanges ('000 subscribers)	1,965,573
Length of Long-distance Optical Cable Lines ('000 km)	890
Broad Band Subscribers Port of Internet ('000 ports)	359,453
Number of IPv4 Addresses ('000)	246,685
International Internet Bandwidth (Mbps)	3,406,824

Telecommunication Services Available at Year-end

Telephone per 100 pop. (Include mobile telephone)	109.9
Telephone Lines per 100 pop.	19.6
Telephone Lines per 100 pop. in Urban Areas	25.2
Mobile Telephone Subscribers per 100 pop.	90.3
Public Telephone lines Per 1,000 Pop.	16.4
Administrative Village with Access to the Internet by Broadband (%)	91.0
Popularization Rate of Internet (%)	45.8

Tourism

Visitor Arrivals

	Thousand
Overseas Visitor Arrivals	129,078
Foreigners	26,290
Chinese Compatriots From Hong Kong and Macao	97,625
Chinese Compatriots From Taiwan Province	5,163
Overnight Tourists	55,686
Chinese Outbound Visitors	98,185
Domestic Visitors	3,262

Composition of Earnings from International Tourism

	Million Dollars
Total	51,664
Transportation	17,457
Sightseeing	3,092
Accommodation	5,976
Food and Beverage	4,128
Shopping	11,182
Entertainment	3,591
Postal and Communication Services	792
Local Transportation	1,444
Other Service	4,001

Domestic Tourism

Domestic Tourists (million person)	3,262
Tourism Expenditure (million yuan)	2,627,610
Per Capita Expenditure (yuan)	806

Overseas Visitor Arrivals by Country/Region

	Thousand
Total	26,290
Asia	16,060
Europe	5,688
Republic of Korea	3,969
Japan	2,878
North America	2,770
Russia	2,186
United States	2,085
Malaysia	1,207
Mongolia	1,050
Philippines	997
Singapore	967
Oceanic and Pacific Islands	863
Australia	723
Canada	684
India	677
Thailand	652
Germany	649
United Kingdom	625
Indonesia	605
Africa	553
France	534
Latin America	354
Italy	251
Korea, D. P. Rep.	207
Netherlands	189
Sweden	159
New Zealand	129
Switzerland	81
Portugal	49
Others	2

Finance

Money Supply

	Billion Yuan
Money Supply (M1)	
Currency in Circulation	5,857
Corporate Demand Deposits	27,872
Money Supply (M2)	
Money Supply (M1)	33,729
Quasi-Money	76,923

Quasi-Money

	Billion Yuan
Corporate Time Deposits	23,270
Personal Savings Deposits	46,703
Other Deposits	6,951

Composition of Social Financing

	Million Yuan
Total of Social Financing	17,316,800
RMB Loans	8,891,600
Foreign Currency Loans	584,800
Credit Loans	2,546,600
Entrusted Loans	1,840,400
Undiscounted Bankers' Acceptances	775,500
Corporate Bonds	1,811,300
Domestic Equity Financing of Non-financial Enterprises	221,900

Official Interest Rates of Deposits of Financial Institutions

	End of 2012, % p.a.
Demand	0.35
Time	
3-Month	2.60
6-Month	2.80
1-Year	3.00
2-Year	3.75
3-Year	4.25
5-Year	4.75

Official Interest Rates of Loans of Financial Institutions

	End of 2012, % p.a.
Short-term	
6-Month	5.60
1-Year	6.00
Medium and Long-term	
3-Year or Less	6.15
5-Year or Less	6.40
Longer than 5-Year	6.55

Gold and Foreign Exchange Reserves

Gold Reserves ('000 oz.)	33,890
Foreign Exchange Reserves (million dollars)	3,821,315

Exchange Rates (Average for the Year)

	Period Average
yuan per $	6.20
yuan per SDR	8.22
yuan per Hong Kong Dollars	0.80
yuan per 100 Japanese Yen	6.33

Balance Sheet of Monetary Authority at Year-end

	Million Yuan
Total Assets	31,727,855
Foreign Assets	27,223,353
Foreign Exchange	26,427,004
Monetary Gold	66,984
Other Foreign Assets	729,366
Claims on Government	1,531,273
Claims on Other Depository Corporations	1,314,790
Claims on Other Financial Corporations	890,736
Claims on Non-financial Sectors	2,499
Other Assets	765,204
Total Liabilities	31,727,855
Reserve Money	27,102,309
Currency Issue	6,498,093
Deposits of Other Depository Corporations	20,604,217
Deposits of Financial Corporations not Included in Reserve Money	133,027
Bond Issue	776,200
Foreign Liabilities	208,827
Deposits of Government	2,861,060
Own Capital	21,975
Other Liabilities	624,457

Balance Sheet of Other Depository Corporations at Year-end

	Million Yuan
Total Assets	152,475,155
Foreign Assets	2,881,409
Reserve Assets	21,177,557
Deposits with Center Bank	20,536,911
Cash in Vault	640,646
Claims on Government	6,234,147
Central Bank Bonds	1,030,142
Claims on Other Depository Corporations	26,044,197
Claims on Other Financial Corporations	7,259,228
Claims on Non-financial Sectors	59,957,515
Claims on Other Resident Sectors	19,686,363
Other Assets	8,204,596
Total Liabilities	152,475,155
Liabilities to Non-financial and Households Institutions	101,277,884
Deposits Included in Broad Money	97,844,431
Corporate Demand Deposits	27,871,661
Corporate Time Deposits	23,269,658
Personal Deposits	46,703,112
Deposits Excluded from Broad Money	2,594,033
Transferable Deposits	745,398
Other Deposits	1,848,635
Other Liabilities	839,420
Liabilities to Central Bank	1,166,321
Liabilities to Other Depository Corporations	11,039,795
Liabilities to Other Financial Corporations	7,480,470
Deposits Included in Broad Money	6,950,623
Foreign Liabilities	1,797,300
Bond Issue	10,367,207

Paid-in Capital	3,254,582
Other Liabilities	16,091,595

Balance Sheet of Foreign-funded Banks at Year-end

	Million Yuan
Total Assets	2,580,500
Foreign Assets	112,800
Reserve Assets	308,300
Deposits with Central Bank	307,300
Cash in Vault	1,000
Claims on Government	153,500
Claims on Central Bank	12,700
Claims on Other Depository Corporations	631,300
Claims on Other Financial Corporations	140,000
Claims on Non-financial Sectors	1,058,100
Claims on Other Resident Sectors	79,000
Other Assets	84,900
Total Liabilities	2,580,500
Liabilities to Non-financial and Households Institutions	1,510,800
Deposits Included in Broad Money	1,212,000
Corporate Demand Deposits	288,700
Corporate Time Deposits	719,300
Personal Deposits	204,000
Deposits Excluded from Broad Money	242,600
Transferable Deposits	115,800
Other Deposits	126,800
Other Liabilities	56,100
Liabilities to Central Bank	100
Liabilities to Other Depository Corporations	122,700

Liabilities to Other Financial Corporations	73,600
Deposits Included in Broad Money	55,200
Foreign Liabilities	526,800
Bond Issue	8,100
Paid-in Capital	158,600
Other Liabilities	179,900

Balance Sheet of Credit Funds of Financial Institutions at Year-end (Funds Uses)

	Million Yuan
Uses of Funds	117,466,617
Total Loans	71,896,146
Domestic Loans	71,708,769
Short-term Loans	29,023,782
Medium and Long-term Loans	39,886,241
Financial Lease	766,083
Bill Financing	1,959,400
Advances	73,263
Overseas Loans	187,376
Portfolio Investments	12,539,938
Shares and Other Investments	4,175,179
Position for Bullion Purchase	66,984
Position for Foreign Exchanges Purchase	28,630,383
Assets with International Financial Institutions	157,987

Government Finance

Main Items of Public Government Revenue of the Central and Local Governments

	Million Yuan
National Government Revenue	12,920,964
Total Tax Revenue	11,053,070
Domestic Value Added Tax	2,881,013
Domestic Consumption Tax	823,132
VAT and Consumption Tax from Imports	1,400,456
VAT and Consumption Tax Rebate for Exports	−1,051,885
Business Tax	1,723,302
Corporate Income Tax	2,242,720
Individual Income Tax	653,153
Resource Tax	100,565
City Maintenance and Construction Tax	341,990
House Property Tax	158,150
Stamp Tax	124,436
Stamp Tax on Security Exchange	46,965
Urban Land Use Tax	171,877
Land Appreciation Tax	329,391
Tax on Vehicles and Boat Operation	47,396
Tax on Ship Tonnages	4,355
Vehicle Purchase Tax	259,634
Tariffs	263,061
Farm Land Occupation Tax	180,823
Deed Tax	384,402
Tobacco Leaf Tax	15,026
Other Tax Revenue	73
Total Non-tax Revenue	1,867,894
Special Program Receipts	352,861

Charge of Administrative and Institutional Units	477,583
Penalty Receipts	165,877
Other Non-tax Receipts	871,573

Main Items of Public Government Revenue of the Central Government

	Million Yuan
National Government Revenue	6,019,848
Total Tax Revenue	5,663,982
Domestic Value Added Tax	2,053,381
Domestic Consumption Tax	823,132
VAT and Consumption Tax from Imports	1,400,456
VAT and Consumption Tax Rebate for Exports	−1,051,885
Business Tax	7,844
Corporate Income Tax	1,444,386
Individual Income Tax	391,899
Resource Tax	4,534
City Maintenance and Construction Tax	17,630
House Property Tax	0
Stamp Tax	45,555
Stamp Tax on Security Exchange	45,555
Urban Land Use Tax	0
Land Appreciation Tax	0
Tax on Vehicles and Boat Operation	0
Tax on Ship Tonnages	4,355
Vehicle Purchase Tax	259,634
Tariffs	263,061
Farm Land Occupation Tax	0
Deed Tax	0
Tobacco Leaf Tax	0

Other Tax Revenue	0
Total Non-tax Revenue	355,866
Special Program Receipts	40,639
Charge of Administrative and Institutional Units	27,848
Penalty Receipts	4,543
Other Non-tax Receipts	282,836

Main Items of Public Government Revenue of the Local Governments

	Million Yuan
National Government Revenue	6,901,116
Total Tax Revenue	5,389,088
Domestic Value Added Tax	827,632
Domestic Consumption Tax	0
VAT and Consumption Tax from Imports	0
VAT and Consumption Tax Rebate for Exports	0
Business Tax	1,715,458
Corporate Income Tax	798,334
Individual Income Tax	261,254
Resource Tax	96,031
City Maintenance and Construction Tax	324,360
House Property Tax	158,150
Stamp Tax	78,881
Stamp Tax on Security Exchange	1,410
Urban Land Use Tax	171,877
Land Appreciation Tax	329,391
Tax on Vehicles and Boat Operation	47,396
Tax on Ship Tonnages	0
Vehicle Purchase Tax	0
Tariffs	0
Farm Land Occupation Tax	180,823

Deed Tax	384,402
Tobacco Leaf Tax	15,026
Other Tax Revenue	73
Total Non-tax Revenue	1,512,028
Special Program Receipts	312,222
Charge of Administrative and Institutional Units	449,735
Penalty Receipts	161,334
Other Non-tax Receipts	588,737

Main Items of Public Government Expenditure of Central and Local Governments

	Million Yuan
Total Expenditure	14,021,210
General Public Services	1,375,513
Foreign Affairs	35,576
National Defense	741,062
Public Security	778,678
Education	2,200,176
Science and Technology	508,430
Culture, Sport and Media	254,439
Social Safety Net and Employment Effort	1,449,054
Medical and Health Care, and Family Planning	827,990
Environment Protection	343,515
Urban and Rural Community Affairs	1,116,557
Agriculture, Forestry and Water Conservancy	1,334,955
Transportation	934,882
Affairs of Exploration, Power and Information	489,906
Affairs of Commerce and Services	136,206
Affairs of Financial Supervision	37,729
Post-earthquake Recovery and Reconstruction	4,279

Other Regional Assistance	15,854
Affairs of Land and Weather	190,612
Affairs of Housing Security	448,055
Affairs of Management of Grain and Oil Reserves	164,942
The Principal and Interest of National Debts	305,621
Other Expenditure	327,179

Main Items of Public Government Expenditure of Central Government

	Million Yuan
Total Expenditure	2,047,176
General Public Services	100,146
Foreign Affairs	35,437
National Defense	717,737
Public Security	129,703
Education	110,665
Science and Technology	236,899
Culture, Sport and Media	20,445
Social Safety Net and Employment Effort	64,082
Medical and Health Care, and Family Planning	7,670
Environment Protection	10,026
Urban and Rural Community Affairs	1,906
Agriculture, Forestry and Water Conservancy	52,691
Transportation	72,299
Affairs of Exploration, Power and Information	45,368
Affairs of Commerce and Services	2,551
Affairs of Financial Supervision	16,432
Post-earthquake Recovery and Reconstruction	0

Other Regional Assistance	0
Affairs of Land and Weather	26,721
Affairs of Housing Security	40,473
Affairs of Management of Grain and Oil Reserves	90,514
The Principal and Interest of National Debts	231,541
Other Expenditure	33,870

Main Items of Public Government Expenditure of Local Governments

	Million Yuan
Total Expenditure	11,974,034
General Public Services	1,275,367
Foreign Affairs	139
National Defense	23,325
Public Security	648,975
Education	2,089,511
Science and Technology	271,531
Culture, Sport and Media	233,994
Social Safety Net and Employment Effort	1,384,972
Medical and Health Care, and Family Planning	820,320
Environment Protection	333,489
Urban and Rural Community Affairs	1,114,651
Agriculture, Forestry and Water Conservancy	1,282,264
Transportation	862,583
Affairs of Exploration, Power and Information	444,538
Affairs of Commerce and Services	133,655
Affairs of Financial Supervision	21,297
Post-earthquake Recovery and Reconstruction	4,279
Other Regional Assistance	15,854
Affairs of Land and Weather	163,891
Affairs of Housing Security	407,582

Affairs of Management of Grain and Oil Reserves	74,428
The Principal and Interest of National Debts	74,080
Other Expenditure	293,309

Outstanding of External Debts

	Million Dollars	%
Total	863,167	100.0
By Type of Debts		
Loans from Foreign Governments	26,515	3.1
Loans from International Financial Institutions	33,280	3.9
International Commercial Loans	466,872	54.1
Trade Loans	336,500	39.0
By Repayment Terms		
Balance of Long-term Debts	186,540	21.6
Balance of Short-term Debts	676,630	78.4

Risk Indicators on External Debts

	%
Debt Service Ratio	1.6
Liability Ratio	9.4
Foreign Debt Ratio	35.6

Prices

Price Index

	Preceding Year = 100
Consumer Price Index	102.6
Retail Price Index	101.4
Producer Price Index for Industrial Products	98.1
Purchasing Price Index for Industrial Producers	98.0
Price Index for Investment in Fixed Assets	100.3

Price Indices of Imports and Exports of Commodity

	Preceding Year = 100
Exports	99.2
Imports	97.6

Income and Expenditure

Average Yearly Wage of Employed Persons in Urban Areas

	Yuan
Total	51,483
Staff and Workers	52,388
State-owned Units	52,657
Urban Collective-owned Units	38,905
Units of Other Types of Ownership	51,453

Ave. Income

	Yuan	%
Disposable Income	18,310.8	100.0
1. Income of Wages and Salaries	10,410.8	56.9
2. Net Business Income	3,434.7	18.8
3. Net Income from Property	1,423.3	7.8
4. Net Income from Transfer	3,042.1	16.6
Cash Disposable Income	17,114.6	100.0
1. Income of Wages and Salaries	10,348.6	60.5
2. Net Business Income	3,354.2	19.6
3. Net Income from Property	526.6	3.1
4. Net Income from Transfer	2,885.2	16.9

Ave. Expenditure

	Yuan	%
Consumption Expenditure	13,220.4	100.0
1. Food, Tobacco and Liquor	4,126.7	31.2
2. Clothing	1,027.1	7.8
3. Residence	2,998.5	22.7

4. Household Facilities, Articles and Services	806.5	6.1
5. Transport and Communications	1,627.1	12.3
6. Education, Cultural and Recreation	1,397.7	10.6
7. Health Care and Medical Services	912.1	6.9
8. Miscellaneous Goods and Services	324.7	2.5
Cash Consumption Expenditure	10,917.4	100.0
1. Food, Tobacco and Liquor	3,822.8	35.0
2. Clothing	1,025.7	9.4
3. Residence	1,155.1	10.6
4. Household Facilities, Articles and Services	801.8	7.3
5. Transport and Communications	1,624.8	14.9
6. Education, Cultural and Recreation	1,396.5	12.8
7. Health Care and Medical Services	772.1	7.1
8. Miscellaneous Goods and Services	318.7	2.9

Main Durable Goods Owned

	Per 100 Households
Cars	16.9
Motorcycle	38.5
Washing Machine	80.8
Refrigerator	82
Microwave Oven	34.6
Color TV	116.1
Air-condition	70.4
Water Heater	64.2
Smoke Exhaust Ventilator	42.5
Telephone Lines	41.6
Mobile Telephone Subscribers	203.2
Computer	48.9
Camera	21

Ave. Consumption of Major Foods

	kg
Grain	148.7
Cereal	138.9
Tuber	2.3
Beans and the Products	7.5
Soybean	1.1
Oil and Fats	12.7
Edible Vegetable Oil	12.0
Vegetable and Mushroom	97.5
Fresh Vegetables	94.9
Products of Meat and Poultry	32.7
Pork	19.8
Beef	1.5
Muttons	0.9
Poultry	6.4
Aquatic Products	10.4
Eggs	8.2
Milk and Dairy Products	11.7
Dried and Fresh Melons and Fruits	40.7
Fresh Melons and Fruits	37.8
Nuts and Processed Products	3.0
Sugar	5.5

Education

Education Expenditure

	2012
Total Funds for Education (¥ billion)	27,696
Government appropriation for education (¥ billion)	22,236
Public expenditure on education (¥ billion)	20,314
Public expenditure on education (% of Public government expenditure)	16.1
Government appropriation for education (% of GDP)	4.3

Teachers and Educational Personnel

	2013
Higher Education	
School	2,491
Educational Personnel	2,296,262
Teachers	1,496,865
Secondary Education	
School	80,797
Educational Personnel	7,569,100
Teachers	5,988,381
Primary Education	
School	235,369
Educational Personnel	5,538,480
Teachers	5,607,283

Enrolment

	2013
Higher Education	
Postgraduates	1,793,953
Doctor's Degree	298,283
Master's Degree	1,495,670
Undergraduate in Regular HEIs	24,680,726
Normal Courses	14,944,353
Short-cycle Courses	9,736,373
Undergraduate in Adult HEIs	6,264,145
Normal Courses	2,654,596
Short-cycle Courses	3,609,549
Web-based Undergraduates	6,146,406
Normal Courses	2,175,100
Short-cycle Courses	3,971,306
Secondary Education	88,582,754
Primary Education	94,848,050

Graduates

	2013
Higher Education	
Postgraduates	513,626
Doctor's Degree	53,139
Master's Degree	460,487
Undergraduate in Regular HEIs	6,387,210
Normal Courses	3,199,716
Short-cycle Courses	3,187,494
Undergraduate in Adult HEIs	1,997,729
Normal Courses	811,159
Short-cycle Courses	1,186,570

Web-based Undergraduates	1,560,762
Normal Courses	536,702
Short-cycle Courses	1,024,060
Secondary Education	30,887,540
Primary Education	16,988,501

Educational Attainment

	Number	%
Population Aged 6 and Over	1,041,825	100.0
No Schooling	52,010	5.0
Primary School	274,658	26.4
Junior Secondary School	425,144	40.8
Senior Secondary School	172,088	16.5
College and Higher Level	117,925	11.3

Illiterate Population Aged 15 and Over by Sex

	%
Illiterate Population to Total Aged 15 and Over	4.60
Male	2.53
Female	6.73

Health

Health Expenditure

	Number
Total Health Expenditure (¥ billion)	3,166.9
Government Health Expenditure (¥ billion)	954.6
% of Total Spending	30.1
Social Health Expenditure (¥ billion)	1,139.4
% of Total Spending	36.0
Out-of-pocket Health Expenditure (¥ billion)	1,072.9
% of Total Spending	33.9
Per Capita Health Expenditure (¥ billion)	2,327.4
Health Spending, % of GDP	5.6

Health Personnel and Hospital Beds

	Number
Doctors per 1,000 pop.	2.04
Nurses per 1,000 pop.	2.04
Hospital Beds ('000)	4578.6
Hospital Beds per 1,000 pop.	3.4

Ranking List of Infectious Diseases Reported

	Number
Viral Hepatitis	1,251,872
Pulmonary Tuberculosis	904,434
Syphilis	406,772
Dysentery	188,669
Gonorrhea	99,659
Brucellosis	43,486

AIDS	42,286
Scarlet Fever	34,207
Measles	27,646
Typhoid and Paratyphoid Fever	14,136
Hemorrhage Fever	12,810
Schistosomiasis	5,699
Dengue Fever	4,663
Malaria	3,896
Encephalitis B	2,178
Pertussis	1,712
Hydrophobia	1,172
Newborn Tetanus	492
Leptospirosis	353
Epidemic Encephalitis	213
Anthrax	193
Cholera	53
HpAI H7N9	19
HpAI	2

Number of Deaths of Classes A and B

	Number
AIDS	11,437
Pulmonary Tuberculosis	2,576
Hydrophobia	1,128
Viral Hepatitis	739
Hemorrhage Fever	109
Syphilis	69
Encephalitis B	64
Newborn Tetanus	45
Measles	24
Epidemic Encephalitis	21
Malaria	20

Dysentery	13
Leptospirosis	5
Typhoid and Paratyphoid Fever	3
Scarlet Fever	2
HpAI	2
Cholera	1
Gonorrhea	1
Anthrax	1
Schistosomiasis	1
HpAI H7N9	1

Mortality Rate of the Maternal and Children Aged under 5 in Surveillance Areas

	‰
Newborn Mortality Rate	6.3
Infant Mortality Rate	9.5
Mortality Rate of Children under 5	12.0
Maternal Mortality Rate	23.2

Resources and Environment

Land Characteristics

	Area (thousand sq. km)	Percentage to Total Area (%)
Total Land Area	9,600.0	100.00
Cultivated Land	1,217.2	12.80
Garden Land	117.9	1.24
Forests Land	2,360.9	24.83
Area of Grassland	2,618.4	27.54
Other Land for Agriculture Use	254.4	2.68
Land for Inhabitation, Mining and Manufacturing	269.2	2.83
Land for Transport Facilities	25.0	0.26
Land for Water Conservancy Facilities	36.5	0.38

Note: Figures were obtained from the Ministry of Land and Resources at year-end of 2008.

Major Rivers[1]

	Drainage Area sq. km	Length km	Annual Flow Million cu. m
Changjiang River (Yangtze River)	1,782,715	6,300	985,700

[1] Figures were obtained from Ministry of Water Resources, and were from the second water resources evaluation between 2002 and 2005.

Huanghe River (Yellow River)	752,773	5,464	59,200
Songhuajiang River	561,222	2,308	81,800
Liaohe River	221,097	1,390	13,700
Zhujiang River (Pearl River)	442,527	2,214	338,100
Haihe River	265,511	1,090	16,300
Huaihe River	268,957	1,000	59,500

Drainage Area of Rivers

	Drainage Area	Percentage to Total
	sq. km	%
Total of Out-flowing Rivers and Inland Rivers	9,506,678	100.00
Out-flowing Rivers	6,150,927	64.70
Heilongjiang River and Suifenhe River	934,802	9.83
Liaohe, Yalujiang and Related Coastal Rivers	314,146	3.30
Haihe River and Luanhe River	320,041	3.37
Huanghe River (Yellow River)	752,773	7.92
Huaihe and Related Coastal Rivers in Shandong Province	330,009	3.47
Changjiang River (Yangtze River)	1,782,715	18.75
Rivers in Zhejiang, Fujian and Taiwan Provinces	244,574	2.57
Zhujiang River (Pearl River) and Related Coastal River	578,974	6.09

Yuanjiang River and Lancang River	240,389	2.53
Nujiang River and West Yunnan Rivers	157,392	1.66
Brahmaputra and Southern Tibet Rivers	387,550	4.08
Western Tibet Rivers	58,783	0.62
Ertix River	48,779	0.51
Inland Rivers	**3,355,751**	**35.30**
Rivers in Inner Mongolia	311,378	3.28
Rivers in Huanghe Upper Reach Area	469,843	4.94
Rivers in Zhunger Basin	323,621	3.40
Rivers in Central Asia	77,757	0.82
Rivers in Tarim Basin	1,079,643	11.36
Rivers in Qinghai Province	321,161	3.38
Rivers in Qiangtang	730,077	7.68
Blind Drainage Areas of Songhua River, Huanghe River and Southern Tibet	42,271	0.44

Water Consumption

	Number
Water Supply (million cu. m)	618,345
Surface Water	500,729
Ground-water	112,622
Others	4,994
Water Use	618,345
Agriculture	392,152
Industry	140,640

Consumption	75,010
Ecological Protection	10,538
Per Capita Water Use (cu. m/person)	456

Ensured Reserves of Major Minerals

	Number
Petroleum ('000 tons)	3,367,328
Natural Gas (million cu. m)	4,642,884
Coal (million tons)	236,290
Iron (Ore, million tons)	19,917
Manganese (Ore, '000 tons)	215,477
Chromium Ore (Ore, '000 tons)	4,015
Vanadium ('000 tons)	9,099
Titanium Ore ('000 tons)	219,570
Copper (Metal, '000 tons)	27,515
Lead (Metal, '000 tons)	15,779
Zinc (Metal, '000 tons)	37,662
Bauxite (Ore, '000 tons)	983,235
Nickel (Metal, '000 tons)	2,535
Tungsten (WO_3, '000 tons)	2,349
Tin (Metal, '000 tons)	1,165
Molybdenum (Metal, '000 tons)	8,067
Antimony (Metal, '000 tons)	460
Gold (Metal, tons)	1,866
Silver (Metal, tons)	37,496
Magnesite Ore (Ore, '000 tons)	1,207,475
Fluorspar Mineral (Mineral, '000 tons)	36,803
Pyrite Ore (Ore, '000 tons)	1,301,941
Phosphorus Ore (Ore, million tons)	3,024
Potassium KCl (KCl, '000 tons)	534,916
Sodium Salt NaCl (NaCl, million tons)	83,019
Mirabilite (Na_2SO_4, million tons)	5,207

Barite Ore (Ore, '000 tons)	39,861
Silicon Materials for Glass Ore (Ore, '000 tons)	1,915,941
Graphite Mineral (Crystal) (Mineral, '000 tons)	53,477
Talc Ore (Ore, '000 tons)	92,739
Kaolin Ore (Ore, '000 tons)	496,497

Main Pollutant Emission in Waste Water

Total Waste Water Discharged ('000 tons)	69,544,327
COD ('000 tons)	23,527
Ammonia Nitrogen ('000 tons)	2,457
Total Nitrogen ('000 tons)	4,481
Total Phosphorus ('000 tons)	487
Petroleum (tons)	18,385
Volatile Phenol (tons)	1,277
Plumbum (kg)	76,112
Mercury (kg)	917
Cadmium (kg)	18,436
Hexavalent Chromium (kg)	58,291
Total Chromium (kg)	163,118
Arsenic (kg)	112,230

Collection, Transport and Disposal of Wastes in Cities

	Thousand Tons
Consumption Wastes Collected and Transported	172,386
Volume of Wastes Disposed	153,940
Collection and Transport of Excrement and Urine	16,824
Disposal of Excrement and Urine	6,778
Treatment Rate of Consumption Wastes (%)	89.3

Main Pollutant Emission in Waste Gas

	Thousand Tons
Sulphur Dioxide	20,439
Nitrogen Oxides	22,274
Smoke and Dust	12,781

Disposal and Utilization of Industrial Solid Wastes

	Thousand Tons
Common Industrial Solid Wastes Produced	3,277,019
Common Industrial Solid Wastes Comprehensively Utilized	2,059,163
Common Industrial Solid Wastes Disposed	829,695
Stock of Common Industrial Solid Wastes	426,342
Common Industrial Solid Wastes Discharged	1,293
Hazardous Wastes Produced	31,569
Hazardous Wastes Utilized	17,001
Hazardous Wastes Disposed	7,012
Stock of Hazardous Wastes	8,109

Area of Wetlands

	Thousand Hectares
Area of Wetlands	536,026
Natural Wetlands	466,747
Man-made Wetlands	67,459
Percentage to Total Area (%)	5.56

Forest Resources

Area of Afforested Land ('000 hectares)	312,590
Forest Area	207,687
Man-made Forest	69,334
Forest Coverage Rate (%)	21.63
Total Standing Forest Stock ('000 cu. m)	16,432,806
Stock Volume of Forest	15,137,297

Principal Natural Protection Statistics

Number	2,697
Area ('000 hectares)	146,310
Percentage to Total Area (%)	14.8

Investment in the Treatment of Environmental Pollution

	Million Yuan
Total Investment	951,650
Investment in Urban Environmental Infrastructure	522,299
Gas Supply	60,790
Centralized Heating	81,948
Drainage Works	105,500
Gardening and Greening	223,486
Environmental Sanitation	50,575
Investment in the Treatment of Industrial Pollution	86,766
Project of Environmental Protection Acceptance Completed This Year	342,584
Total Investment in the Treatment of Environmental Pollution as Percent of GDP (%)	1.67

Investment Completed in the Treatment of Industrial Pollution

	Million Yuan
Total	86,766
Waste Water	12,488
Waste Gas	64,091
Solid Waste	1,405
Noise Pollution	176
Other Pollution	8,606

Energy

Composition of Energy Output

Total Output (m tons of SCE)	3,400.0
	% of Total Output
Coal	75.6
Crude Oil	8.9
Natural Gas	4.6
Hydro-power, Nuclear Power, Wind Power	10.9

Composition of Energy Consumption

Total Consumption (m tons of SCE)	3,750.0
	% of Total Consumption
Coal	66.0
Crude Oil	18.4
Natural Gas	5.8
Hydro-power, Nuclear Power, Wind Power	9.8

Energy Balance

	M. Tons of SCE, 2012
Total Energy Available for Consumption	3,786.9
Primary Energy Output	3,318.5
Imports	666.0
Exports (−)	73.8
Stock Changes in the Year	−123.8
Total Energy Consumption	3,617.3
Balance	169.6

Petroleum Balance

	M. Tons, 2012
Total Energy Available for Consumption 2012	478.6
Output	207.5
Imports	330.9
Exports (−)	38.8
Stock Changes in the Year	−20.9
Total Energy Consumption	476.5
Balance	2.1

Coal Balance

	M. Tons, 2012
Total Energy Available for Consumption 2012	3,800.3
Output	3,645.0
Imports	288.4
Exports (−)	9.3
Stock Changes in the Year	−123.8
Total Energy Consumption	3,526.5
Balance	273.9

Electricity Balance

	bn Kwh, 2012
Total Energy Available for Consumption 2012	4,976.8
Output	4,987.6
Hydropower	872.1
Thermal Power	3,892.8
Nuclear Power	97.4
Wind Power	96.0
Exports (−)	6.9
Stock Changes in the Year	17.7
Total Energy Consumption	4,976.3

Efficiency of Energy Conversion

	%, 2012
Total Efficiency	72.4
Electricity Generation and Heating by Power Stations	43.0
Coking	94.6
Petroleum Refining	97.0

Average Daily Consumption

	2012
Total ('000 tons of SCE)	9,910.5
Coal ('000 tons)	9,661.6
Coke ('000 tons)	1,078.7
Crude Oil ('000 tons)	1,278.9
Fuel Oil ('000 tons)	100.9
Gasoline ('000 tons)	223.0
Kerosene ('000 tons)	53.6
Diesel Oil ('000 tons)	464.8
Natural Gas (m cu. m)	400.8
Electricity (m kwh)	13,633.6

Annual per Capita Energy Consumption of Households 2012

	2012
Total (kg of SCE)	293.8
Coal (kg)	67.8
Kerosene (kg)	0.1
Liquefied Petroleum Gas (kg)	12.1
Natural Gas (cu. m)	21.3
Coal Gas (cu. m)	10.2
Electricity (kwh)	460.4

Culture and Recreation

Basic Statistics on Radio and Television Industry

Radio

Radio Coverage Rate of the Population (%)	97.8
Number of Radio Programs	2,644
Public Radio	2,637
Pay Radio	7
Length of Public Radio Programs Broadcasted ('000 hours)	13,795
Length of Radio Programs Produced ('000 hours)	7,391

Television

TV Coverage Rate of the Population (%)	98.4
Users of Cable Radio and TV ('000 households)	228,938
Users of Digital TV	171,597
Popularization Rate of Cable Radio and TV (%)	54.1
Number of TV Programs	3,338
Public TV	3,250
Pay TV	88
Length of Public TV Programs Broadcasted ('000 hours)	17,057
Number of TV Plays Broadcasted (series)	240,996
Imported TV Plays	3,616
Number of TV Plays Broadcasted (episodes)	6,614,157
Imported TV Plays	98,939
Number of Cartoons Broadcasted (hours)	293,139
Imported Cartoons	14,014
Length of TV Programs Produced	3,397,912

Movies

State-owned Movie Studios	38
Feature Film Studios	31

Movie Circuit (line)	42
Movie Screen (unit)	18,195
Domestic Movie Box Office Revenue	218
Chinese Movies	128
Imported Movies	90

TV Technology and Others

Revenue of Radio and TV (million yuan)	373,488
Staff and Workers of Radio and TV ('000 persons)	844
Transmission and Relaying Stations of Medium and Short Wave Broadcast	850
Relaying Stations of Frequency Modulation Broadcasting	10,334
TV Transmission and Relaying Stations	13,365
Microwave Stations	2,207

Number of Books, Magazines and Newspapers Published

	Number
Books Published	
Number of Publications	444,427
Printed Copies (million copies)	8,310
Printed Sheets (million sheets)	71,260
Magazines Published	
Number of Publications	9,877
Average Printed Copies per Issue ('000 copies)	164,535
Total Printed Copies (million copies)	3,272
Printed Sheets (million sheets)	19,470
Newspapers Published	
Number of Publications	1,915
Average Printed Copies per Issue ('000 copies)	236,958
Total Printed Copies (million copies)	48,240
Printed Sheets (million sheets)	209,784

Utilization of Cultural Facilities

	Number
Public Libraries	3,112
Cultural Centers	44,260
Museums	3,473
Art Performance Troupes	8,180
Art Performance Places	1,344

Principal Arts Statistics

	Numbers
Art Performance Troupes	
Number of Institutions	8,180
Number of Performances ('000 shows)	1,651
Number of Domestic Audience	900,643
Art Performance Places	
Number of Institutions	1,344
Number of Performances ('000 shows)	829
Number of Audience	77,763

Number of Institutions of Physical Education System

	Number
Total	7,089
Administrative Agencies of Physical Culture and Sports	3,025
Sports Events Management	300
Colleges	7
Sports Technical Institutes	20
Physical Education and Sports Schools	268
Competitive Sports School	16

Spare-time Sports School	1,460
Physical Education and Sports Schools	23
Secondary Schools of Physical Education	30
Training Bases	80
Stadium and Gymnasium	676
Science and Technology Institute	57
Other Institutions	1,011
Others	116

Public Security

Criminal Cases Registered in Public Security Organs

	Number	%
Total	6,598,247	100
Homicide	10,640	0.16
Injury	161,910	2.45
Robbery	146,193	2.22
Rape	34,102	0.52
Abducting Women or Children	20,735	0.31
Larceny	4,506,414	68.30
Fraud	676,771	10.26
Smuggling	1,853	0.03
Forging Currency, Selling, Buying, Transporting, Holding and Using Counterfeit Currency	768	0.01
Others	1,038,861	15.74

Cases of Offence Against Public Order Accepted to be Treated by Public Security Organs

	Number
Total	13,307,501
Disturbing Business Orders	130,652
Disturbing the Orders in Public Places	464,682
Causing Quarrels and Making Troubles	90,037
Obstructing Government Workers in Performing Their Duties	33,229
Violation of Firearms Control Regulations	63,802
Violation of Explosives Control Regulations	19,579
Battering Other Persons	4,119,105

Willfully Injuring Others	294,449
Stealing Property	2,161,720
Extortion and Blackmail	16,079
Robbery and Snatch	30,111
Stealing and Damaging Public Facilities	12,573
Forge/alter/scalp Valuable Coupons or Certificates	7,174
Violating the Hotel Management Regulations	135,868
Violating the Rent Control Regulations	208,415
Swindling, Seizing and Extorting Property	317,701
Prostitution or Soliciting Prostitutes	84,375
Gambling	393,829
Illegal Drug Related Action	540,306
Others	4,183,815

Cases of Offence Against Public Order Investigated and Treated by Public Security Organs

	Number
Total	12,746,493
Disturbing Business Orders	128,897
Disturbing the Orders in Public Places	460,004
Causing Quarrels and Making Troubles	85,183
Obstructing Government Workers in Performing Their Duties	32,566
Violation of Firearms Control Regulations	63,015
Violation of Explosives Control Regulations	19,088
Battering Other Persons	3,992,598
Willfully Injuring Others	277,698
Stealing Property	1,920,436
Extortion and Blackmail	14,137
Robbery and Snatch	24,768
Stealing and Damaging Public Facilities	11,239
Forge/alter/scalp Valuable Coupons or Certificates	7,050

Violating the Hotel Management Regulations	134,759
Violating the Rent Control Regulations	207,604
Swindling, Seizing and Extorting Property	271,918
Prostitution or Soliciting Prostitutes	83,891
Gambling	390,697
Illegal Drug Related Action	536,691
Others	4,084,254

Cases of Offence Against Public Order Accepted by Public Security Organs

	Per 10,000 Population
Total	97.33
Disturbing Business Orders	0.96
Disturbing the Orders in Public Places	3.40
Causing Quarrels and Making Troubles	0.66
Obstructing Government Workers in Performing Their Duties	0.24
Violation of Firearms Control Regulations	0.47
Violation of Explosives Control Regulations	0.14
Battering Other Persons	30.13
Willfully Injuring Others	2.15
Stealing Property	15.81
Extortion and Blackmail	0.12
Robbery and Snatch	0.22
Stealing and Damaging Public Facilities	0.09
Forge/alter/scalp Valuable Coupons or Certificates	0.05
Violating the Hotel Management Regulations	0.99
Violating the Rent Control Regulations	1.52
Swindling, Seizing and Extorting Property	2.32
Prostitution or Soliciting Prostitutes	0.62
Gambling	2.88

Illegal Drug Related Action	3.95
Others	32.60

Number and Direct Property Losses of Traffic Accidents

	Number	Thousand Yuan
Total	198,394	1,038,966
Serious Accidents	16	2,585
Extraordinarily Serious Accidents	0	0
Vehicles	183,404	1,000,341
Motor Vehicles	138,113	902,671
Motorcycles	40,858	76,430
Tractors	3,093	8,649
Non-motor-driven Vehicles	12,839	23,688
Bicycles	1,304	3,164
Pedestrians and Passengers	2,088	14,795
Others	63	142

Deaths and Injuries in Traffic Accidents

	Deaths	Injuries
Total	58,539	213,724
Serious Accidents	208	259
Extraordinarily Serious Accidents	0	0
Vehicles	55,316	198,317
Motor Vehicles	42,927	143,672
Motorcycles	10,463	50,635
Tractors	1,259	2,833
Non-motor-driven Vehicles	2,019	14,261
Bicycles	300	1,209
Pedestrians and Passengers	1185	1,086
Others	19	60

Part 2

Province Rankings

Population: Size and Growth

Largest Populations

Million

1	Guangdong	106.4	9	Hubei	58.0
2	Shandong	97.3	10	Zhejiang	55.0
3	Henan	94.1	11	Guangxi	47.2
4	Sichuan	81.1	12	Yunnan	46.9
5	Jiangsu	79.4	13	Jiangxi	45.2
6	Hebei	73.3	14	Liaoning	43.9
7	Hunan	66.9	15	Heilongjiang	38.4
8	Anhui	60.3	16	Fujian	37.7

Largest Urban Populations

Highest, %

1	Shanghai	89.60	9	Inner Mongolia	58.71
2	Beijing	86.30	10	Chongqing	58.34
3	Tianjin	82.01	11	Heilongjiang	57.40
4	Guangdong	67.76	12	Hubei	54.51
5	Liaoning	66.45	13	Jilin	54.20
6	Jiangsu	64.11	14	Shandong	53.75
7	Zhejiang	64.00	15	Hainan	52.74
8	Fujian	60.77	16	Shanxi	52.56

Natural Growth Rate

Highest, ‰

1	Xinjiang	10.92	9	Hunan	6.54
2	Tibet	10.38	10	Fujian	6.19
3	Hainan	8.69	11	Hebei	6.17

4	Ningxia	8.62	12	Yunnan	6.17
5	Qinghai	8.03	13	Gansu	6.08
6	Guangxi	7.93	14	Guangdong	6.02
7	Jiangxi	6.91	15	Guizhou	5.90
8	Anhui	6.82	16	Henan	5.51

Crude Birth Rates

Highest, ‰

1	Xinjiang	15.84	9	Guizhou	13.05
2	Tibet	15.77	10	Hebei	13.04
3	Hainan	14.59	11	Anhui	12.88
4	Guangxi	14.28	12	Yunnan	12.60
5	Qinghai	14.16	13	Henan	12.27
6	Hunan	13.50	14	Fujian	12.20
7	Jiangxi	13.19	15	Gansu	12.16
8	Ningxia	13.12	16	Shandong	11.41

Crude Death Rates

Lowest, ‰

1	Ningxia	4.50	9	Shanxi	5.57
2	Beijing	4.52	10	Inner Mongolia	5.62
3	Guangdong	4.69	11	Hainan	5.90
4	Xinjiang	4.92	12	Tianjin	6.00
5	Jilin	5.04	13	Fujian	6.01
6	Shanghai	5.24	14	Anhui	6.06
7	Tibet	5.39	15	Gansu	6.08
8	Zhejiang	5.45	16	Heilongjiang	6.08

Average Family Size

Largest, Person/Household

1	Tibet	4.05	9	Henan	3.28
2	Hainan	3.52	10	Hunan	3.25
3	Jiangxi	3.42	11	Ningxia	3.20
4	Qinghai	3.37	12	Hebei	3.17
5	Gansu	3.35	13	Guangdong	3.15
6	Guangxi	3.31	14	Guizhou	3.07
7	Xinjiang	3.30	15	Shaanxi	3.05
8	Yunnan	3.28	16	Anhui	3.03

Population: Matters of Breeding and Sex

Gross Dependency Ratio

Highest, %

1	Guizhou	45.70	9	Tibet	39.73
2	Guangxi	44.43	10	Yunnan	38.96
3	Henan	42.23	11	Ningxia	37.59
4	Sichuan	41.46	12	Xinjiang	37.36
5	Anhui	40.83	13	Qinghai	37.06
6	Chongqing	40.55	14	Hebei	36.92
7	Hunan	40.53	15	Hainan	36.79
8	Jiangxi	40.26	16	Shandong	35.98

Children Dependency Ratio

Highest, %

1	Tibet	32.50	9	Qinghai	27.24
2	Guizhou	32.19	10	Anhui	26.00
3	Guangxi	31.01	11	Hunan	25.67
4	Henan	29.54	12	Hainan	25.64
5	Xinjiang	28.61	13	Hebei	24.37
6	Ningxia	27.86	14	Sichuan	23.41
7	Yunnan	27.83	15	Gansu	22.78
8	Jiangxi	27.63	16	Fujian	22.48

Old Dependency Ratio

Highest, %

1	Chongqing	18.62	9	Guangxi	13.42
2	Sichuan	18.05	10	Shanghai	13.30
3	Jiangsu	16.47	11	Hubei	13.18

4	Shandong	14.93	12	Shaanxi	13.09
5	Hunan	14.85	13	Liaoning	12.87
6	Anhui	14.83	14	Henan	12.70
7	Tianjin	14.81	15	Jiangxi	12.63
8	Guizhou	13.52	16	Hebei	12.55

Largest Sex Ratio

Female = 100

1	Hainan	111.71	9	Zhejiang	107.54
2	Guangdong	110.84	10	Guizhou	107.05
3	Guangxi	109.44	11	Shanghai	106.24
4	Jiangxi	108.52	12	Jilin	106.23
5	Inner Mongolia	107.91	13	Hunan	105.70
6	Fujian	107.89	14	Gansu	105.64
7	Beijing	107.62	15	Shanxi	105.52
8	Yunnan	107.56	16	Hebei	105.50

Illiterate Population Aged 15 and Over

Highest, %

1	Tibet	41.18	9	Zhejiang	5.38
2	Qinghai	13.53	10	Shandong	5.31
3	Guizhou	10.44	11	Hubei	5.30
4	Yunnan	8.45	12	Fujian	5.06
5	Ningxia	7.88	13	Henan	4.88
6	Anhui	7.43	14	Chongqing	4.81
7	Gansu	7.39	15	Hainan	4.76
8	Sichuan	6.67	16	Shaanxi	4.29

Biggest Population Living in Urban Areas

Highest, %

1	Shanghai	89.6	9	Inner Mongolia	58.7
2	Beijing	86.3	10	Chongqing	58.3
3	Tianjin	82.0	11	Heilongjiang	57.4
4	Guangdong	67.8	12	Hubei	54.5
5	Liaoning	66.5	13	Jilin	54.2
6	Jiangsu	64.1	14	Shandong	53.8
7	Zhejiang	64.0	15	Hainan	52.7
8	Fujian	60.8	16	Shanxi	52.6

Workers in Urban Area

Highest Unemployment Rate in Urban Area

%, 2013

1	Heilongjiang	4.4	9	Inner Mongolia	3.7
2	Hunan	4.2	10	Tianjin	3.6
3	Sichuan	4.1	11	Fujian	3.6
4	Ningxia	4.1	12	Hubei	3.5
5	Shanghai	4.0	13	Anhui	3.4
6	Yunnan	4.0	14	Chongqing	3.4
7	Jilin	3.7	15	Xinjiang	3.4
8	Hebei	3.7	16	Liaoning	3.4

Highest Average Wage of Employed Persons in Urban Area

Yuan

1	Beijing	93,006	9	Inner Mongolia	50,723
2	Shanghai	90,908	10	Ningxia	50,476
3	Tianjin	67,773	11	Chongqing	50,006
4	Tibet	57,773	12	Xinjiang	49,064
5	Jiangsu	57,177	13	Fujian	48,538
6	Zhejiang	56,571	14	Sichuan	47,965
7	Guangdong	53,318	15	Anhui	47,806
8	Qinghai	51,393	16	Shaanxi	47,446

National Economy

Biggest Economies

GDP, Billion Yuan

1	Guangdong	6,216		9	Hubei	2,467
2	Jiangsu	5,916		10	Hunan	2,450
3	Shandong	5,468		11	Fujian	2,176
4	Zhejiang	3,757		12	Shanghai	2,160
5	Henan	3,216		13	Beijing	1,950
6	Hebei	2,830		14	Anhui	1,904
7	Liaoning	2,708		15	Inner Mongolia	1,683
8	Sichuan	2,626		16	Shaanxi	1,605

Highest GDP per Head

Yuan

1	Tianjin	99,607		9	Fujian	57,856
2	Beijing	93,213		10	Shandong	56,323
3	Shanghai	90,092		11	Jilin	47,191
4	Jiangsu	74,607		12	Chongqing	42,795
5	Zhejiang	68,462		13	Shaanxi	42,692
6	Inner Mongolia	67,498		14	Hubei	42,613
7	Liaoning	61,686		15	Ningxia	39,420
8	Guangdong	58,540		16	Hebei	38,716

Largest Agriculture Output

Billion Yuan

1	Shandong	474		9	Heilongjiang	252
2	Henan	406		10	Anhui	235
3	Jiangsu	365		11	Guangxi	234

4	Hebei	350	12	Liaoning	232
5	Sichuan	343	13	Fujian	194
6	Hunan	310	14	Yunnan	190
7	Hubei	310	15	Zhejiang	178
8	Guangdong	305	16	Jiangxi	164

Largest Industry Output

Billion Yuan

1	Guangdong	2,943	9	Hubei	1,217
2	Jiangsu	2,909	10	Hunan	1,152
3	Shandong	2,742	11	Fujian	1,132
4	Zhejiang	1,845	12	Anhui	1,040
5	Henan	1,781	13	Inner Mongolia	908
6	Hebei	1,476	14	Shaanxi	891
7	Liaoning	1,427	15	Shanghai	803
8	Sichuan	1,358	16	Jiangxi	767

Largest Services Output

Billion Yuan

1	Guangdong	2,969	9	Hebei	1,004
2	Jiangsu	2,642	10	Hunan	989
3	Shandong	2,252	11	Hubei	940
4	Zhejiang	1,734	12	Sichuan	926
5	Beijing	1,499	13	Fujian	851
6	Shanghai	1,345	14	Tianjin	691
7	Liaoning	1,049	15	Anhui	629
8	Henan	1,029	16	Inner Mongolia	615

Economic Growth

Highest Economic Growth

Annual % increase in real GDP, 2013

1	Tianjin	12.5	9	Gansu	10.8
2	Guizhou	12.5	10	Qinghai	10.8
3	Chongqing	12.3	11	Anhui	10.4
4	Yunnan	12.1	12	Guangxi	10.2
5	Tibet	12.1	13	Jiangxi	10.1
6	Fujian	11	14	Hubei	10.1
7	Shaanxi	11	15	Hunan	10.1
8	Xinjiang	11	16	Sichuan	10

Highest Industry Growth

Average annual % increase in real terms, 2013

1	Tibet	20.0	9	Ningxia	12.5
2	Guizhou	14.1	10	Anhui	12.4
3	Xinjiang	13.6	11	Qinghai	12.3
4	Chongqing	13.4	12	Guangxi	11.9
5	Yunnan	13.3	13	Jiangxi	11.7
6	Fujian	12.9	14	Gansu	11.5
7	Tianjin	12.7	15	Sichuan	11.5
8	Shaanxi	12.6	16	Hubei	11.3

Highest Services Growth

Annual % increase in real terms, 2013

1	Guizhou	12.6	9	Guangxi	10.2
2	Tianjin	12.5	10	Hubei	10
3	Yunnan	12.4	11	Guangdong	9.9
4	Hainan	12.1	12	Sichuan	9.9

5	Chongqing	12	13	Shaanxi	9.9
6	Gansu	11.5	14	Jiangsu	9.8
7	Hunan	11.4	15	Qinghai	9.8
8	Heilongjiang	10.4	16	Fujian	9.6

Highest Gross Capital Formation

Billion Yuan

1	Shandong	3,095	9	Hubei	1,425
2	Jiangsu	2,863	10	Hunan	1,400
3	Guangdong	2,605	11	Sichuan	1,349
4	Henan	2,483	12	Fujian	1,280
5	Zhejiang	1,711	13	Tianjin	1,105
6	Liaoning	1,694	14	Shaanxi	1,104
7	Hebei	1,639	15	Guangxi	1,013
8	Inner Mongolia	1,573	16	Yunnan	996

Highest Final Consumption Expenditure

Billion Yuan

1	Guangdong	3,220	9	Hebei	1,189
2	Jiangsu	2,642	10	Hunan	1,128
3	Shandong	2,260	11	Liaoning	1,121
4	Zhejiang	1,774	12	Hubei	1,116
5	Henan	1,529	13	Anhui	919
6	Sichuan	1,322	14	Fujian	839
7	Shanghai	1,252	15	Heilongjiang	796
8	Beijing	1,195	16	Guangxi	741

Investment in Fixed Assets

Total Investment in Fixed Assets

Million Yuan

1	Shandong	3,678,907	9	Hubei	1,930,733
2	Jiangsu	3,637,332	10	Anhui	1,862,190
3	Henan	2,608,746	11	Hunan	1,784,140
4	Liaoning	2,510,766	12	Fujian	1,532,744
5	Hebei	2,319,423	13	Shaanxi	1,488,415
6	Guangdong	2,230,839	14	Inner Mongolia	1,421,738
7	Zhejiang	2,078,211	15	Jiangxi	1,285,025
8	Sichuan	2,032,611	16	Guangxi	1,190,767

Hong Kong, Macao and Taiwan Investment in Fixed Assets

Million Yuan

1	Jiangsu	160,550	9	Sichuan	33,776
2	Guangdong	159,070	10	Shanghai	30,189
3	Liaoning	116,982	11	Anhui	28,786
4	Zhejiang	112,659	12	Hubei	24,107
5	Fujian	82,129	13	Jiangxi	24,063
6	Shandong	61,733	14	Hebei	21,619
7	Chongqing	45,306	15	Henan	21,265
8	Beijing	45,143	16	Hainan	20,764

Foreign Investment in Fixed Assets

Million Yuan

1	Jiangsu	231,438	9	Hebei	39,082
2	Guangdong	129,254	10	Hubei	37,653
3	Liaoning	93,049	11	Shaanxi	34,874
4	Zhejiang	75,764	12	Tianjin	33,001
5	Shandong	64,252	13	Chongqing	32,549
6	Shanghai	61,129	14	Beijing	31,148
7	Fujian	46,196	15	Anhui	30,034
8	Sichuan	43,048	16	Henan	24,544

Agriculture

Largest Agriculture Output

Million Yuan

1	Shandong	874,999	9	Heilongjiang	463,326
2	Henan	719,808	10	Liaoning	434,972
3	Jiangsu	615,803	11	Anhui	400,924
4	Hebei	583,294	12	Guangxi	375,519
5	Sichuan	562,027	13	Fujian	328,196
6	Hubei	516,056	14	Yunnan	305,604
7	Hunan	504,358	15	Zhejiang	283,739
8	Guangdong	494,681	16	Inner Mongolia	269,950

Most Economically Dependent on Agriculture

% of GDP from Agriculture

1	Hainan	24.0	9	Henan	12.6
2	Xinjiang	17.6	10	Hubei	12.6
3	Heilongjiang	17.5	11	Hunan	12.6
4	Guangxi	16.3	12	Hebei	12.4
5	Yunnan	16.2	13	Anhui	12.3
6	Gansu	14.0	14	Jilin	11.6
7	Sichuan	13.0	15	Jiangxi	11.4
8	Guizhou	12.9	16	Tibet	10.7

Biggest Producers of Farm Products

Cereal

Thousand Tons

1	Henan	55,227	9	Hunan	27,635
2	Heilongjiang	54,959	10	Inner Mongolia	24,336
3	Shandong	42,971	11	Hubei	23,739

4	Jilin	34,438	12	Liaoning	21,227
5	Jiangsu	33,130	13	Jiangxi	20,199
6	Hebei	32,218	14	Yunnan	14,850
7	Anhui	31,273	15	Guangxi	14,255
8	Sichuan	28,153	16	Xinjiang	13,397

Beans

Thousand Tons

1	Heilongjiang	4,002	9	Chongqing	460
2	Inner Mongolia	1,383	10	Shandong	404
3	Yunnan	1,314	11	Gansu	379
4	Anhui	1,140	12	Hunan	354
5	Sichuan	921	13	Zhejiang	338
6	Henan	788	14	Shaanxi	328
7	Jiangsu	722	15	Hubei	317
8	Jilin	588	16	Liaoning	313

Tubers

Thousand Tons

1	Sichuan	4,797	9	Hunan	1,268
2	Chongqing	2,974	10	Fujian	1,193
3	Guizhou	2,634	11	Hebei	1,124
4	Gansu	2,446	12	Henan	1,121
5	Yunnan	2,076	13	Heilongjiang	1,080
6	Inner Mongolia	2,011	14	Hubei	957
7	Shandong	1,906	15	Shaanxi	868
8	Guangdong	1,659	16	Guangxi	730

Cottons

Thousand Tons

1	Xinjiang	3,518	9	Jiangxi	131
2	Shandong	621	10	Gansu	71
3	Hubei	460	11	Shaanxi	58
4	Hebei	457	12	Tianjin	48
5	Anhui	251	13	Shanxi	31
6	Jiangsu	209	14	Zhejiang	28
7	Hunan	198	15	Sichuan	13
8	Henan	190	16	Jilin	6

Oil-bearing Crops

Thousand Tons

1	Henan	5,891	9	Jiangsu	1,504
2	Shandong	3,496	10	Jiangxi	1,193
3	Hubei	3,332	11	Liaoning	1,136
4	Sichuan	2,904	12	Guangdong	1,010
5	Anhui	2,254	13	Guizhou	915
6	Hunan	2,244	14	Jilin	840
7	Inner Mongolia	1,581	15	Gansu	697
8	Hebei	1,511	16	Yunnan	607

Fiber Crops

Thousand Tons

1	Sichuan	56.1	9	Jiangxi	8.1
2	Henan	36.5	10	Yunnan	7.9
3	Anhui	26.6	11	Guangxi	7.5
4	Hubei	26.1	12	Gansu	3.4
5	Hunan	16.9	13	Jiangsu	1.9
6	Xinjiang	14.7	14	Hainan	1.2

| 7 | Chongqing | 9.5 | 15 | Guizhou | 1.0 |
| 8 | Heilongjiang | 9.2 | 16 | Hebei | 0.8 |

Sugarcane

Thousand Tons

1	Guangxi	81,043	9	Fujian	586
2	Yunnan	21,463	10	Sichuan	569
3	Guangdong	15,532	11	Hubei	287
4	Hainan	4,408	12	Henan	283
5	Guizhou	1,593	13	Anhui	202
6	Hunan	737	14	Chongqing	109
7	Jiangxi	646	15	Jiangsu	95
8	Zhejiang	639	16	Shanghai	7

Beetroots

Thousand Tons

1	Xinjiang	4,764.66	9	Sichuan	1.89
2	Inner Mongolia	1,813.61	10	Jiangsu	0.20
3	Heilongjiang	1,231.73	11	Qinghai	0.15
4	Hebei	742.42	12	Shandong	0.07
5	Gansu	247.22	13	Hubei	0.05
6	Shanxi	224.57	14	Guizhou	0.03
7	Liaoning	171.22	15	Shaanxi	0.01
8	Jilin	61.99			

Tobacco

Thousand Tons

1	Yunnan	1,076	9	Chongqing	97
2	Guizhou	436	10	Heilongjiang	89
3	Henan	347	11	Shaanxi	87

4	Hunan	263	12	Jilin	61
5	Sichuan	251	13	Guangdong	57
6	Fujian	163	14	Jiangxi	51
7	Hubei	127	15	Anhui	43
8	Shandong	112	16	Guangxi	38

Silkworm Cocoons

Thousand Tons

1	Guangxi	323.4	9	Yunnan	28.1
2	Sichuan	112.9	10	Henan	25.1
3	Guangdong	102.0	11	Chongqing	18.2
4	Jiangsu	59.0	12	Shaanxi	13.4
5	Zhejiang	55.2	13	Hubei	7.7
6	Liaoning	51.8	14	Inner Mongolia	7.7
7	Anhui	32.2	15	Jiangxi	6.9
8	Shandong	31.0	16	Shanxi	6.2

Tea

Thousand Tons

1	Fujian	347.0	9	Guangdong	69.8
2	Yunnan	301.7	10	Henan	55.9
3	Hubei	222.0	11	Guangxi	53.9
4	Sichuan	219.5	12	Jiangxi	43.1
5	Zhejiang	168.6	13	Shaanxi	40.7
6	Hunan	146.0	14	Chongqing	34.2
7	Anhui	100.9	15	Shandong	15.7
8	Guizhou	89.4	16	Jiangsu	13.9

Fruits

Thousand Tons

1	Shandong	30,288	9	Hubei	9,205
2	Henan	25,997	10	Anhui	9,051
3	Hebei	18,633	11	Hunan	8,794
4	Shaanxi	17,644	12	Sichuan	8,401
5	Guangdong	14,854	13	Jiangsu	8,142
6	Guangxi	14,334	14	Fujian	7,443
7	Xinjiang	13,269	15	Zhejiang	7,157
8	Liaoning	9,447	16	Shanxi	7,118

Biggest Producers of Forest Products

Timber

Thousand cu. m

1	Guangxi	22,880	9	Jiangxi	2,669
2	Guangdong	8,091	10	Hubei	2,519
3	Fujian	5,723	11	Henan	2,431
4	Shandong	5,591	12	Sichuan	2,371
5	Anhui	4,775	13	Heilongjiang	2,196
6	Hunan	4,749	14	Inner Mongolia	1,862
7	Yunnan	4,302	15	Guizhou	1,809
8	Jilin	3,474	16	Liaoning	1,783

Pine Resin

Tons

1	Guangxi	586,484	9	Anhui	11,141
2	Guangdong	216,098	10	Guizhou	7,631
3	Yunnan	182,369	11	Henan	3,064
4	Jiangxi	101,314	12	Sichuan	1,987
5	Fujian	100,413	13	Zhejiang	1,136

6	Hunan	41,041	14	Shaanxi	797
7	Hubei	39,867	15	Chongqing	57
8	Hainan	14,348			

Lacquer

Tons

1	Hubei	6,897	9	Yunnan	271
2	Chongqing	6,095	10	Jiangxi	235
3	Shaanxi	4,476	11	Fujian	178
4	Guizhou	3,103	12	Guangxi	37
5	Henan	2,209	13	Gansu	34
6	Hunan	610	14	Zhejiang	10
7	Sichuan	583	15	Guangdong	6
8	Anhui	410			

Tung-oil Seeds

Tons

1	Henan	83,830	9	Sichuan	15,276
2	Guangxi	77,715	10	Chongqing	13,412
3	Guizhou	75,275	11	Jiangxi	8,012
4	Hunan	39,591	12	Guangdong	7,650
5	Shaanxi	28,390	13	Anhui	2,830
6	Hubei	25,290	14	Zhejiang	87
7	Fujian	23,240	15	Gansu	49
8	Yunnan	18,277			

Tea-oil Seeds

Tons

1	Hunan	725,190	9	Guizhou	41,430
2	Jiangxi	412,339	10	Henan	17,461
3	Guangxi	168,544	11	Yunnan	15,390

4	Fujian	97,825	12	Shaanxi	7,694
5	Hubei	87,483	13	Sichuan	5,361
6	Guangdong	83,547	14	Chongqing	4,520
7	Anhui	63,932	15	Jiangsu	62
8	Zhejiang	45,681	16	Hainan	47

Rubber

Tons

1	Yunnan	425,604	3	Guangdong	17,387
2	Hainan	420,816	4	Guangxi	999

Biggest Producers of Livestock Products

Meat

Thousand Tons

1	Shandong	7,748	9	Guangxi	4,200
2	Henan	6,991	10	Anhui	4,038
3	Sichuan	6,904	11	Jiangsu	3,832
4	Hunan	5,192	12	Yunnan	3,594
5	Hebei	4,488	13	Jiangxi	3,219
6	Guangdong	4,352	14	Jilin	2,627
7	Hubei	4,301	15	Inner Mongolia	2,449
8	Liaoning	4,201	16	Heilongjiang	2,213

Milk

Thousand Tons

1	Inner Mongolia	7,786	9	Ningxia	1,042
2	Heilongjiang	5,225	10	Shanxi	872
3	Hebei	4,657	11	Sichuan	711
4	Henan	3,288	12	Tianjin	685
5	Shandong	2,812	13	Beijing	615

6	Shaanxi	1,885	14	Jiangsu	599
7	Xinjiang	1,392	15	Yunnan	593
8	Liaoning	1,257	16	Jilin	483

Sheep Wool

Tons

1	Inner Mongolia	110,532	9	Shandong	9,640
2	Xinjiang	91,620	10	Ningxia	9,237
3	Hebei	33,105	11	Henan	8,263
4	Heilongjiang	32,129	12	Shanxi	8,185
5	Gansu	29,991	13	Tibet	8,028
6	Jilin	18,972	14	Shaanxi	6,854
7	Qinghai	17,928	15	Sichuan	6,106
8	Liaoning	14,988	16	Zhejiang	1,972

Goat Wool

Tons

1	Inner Mongolia	10,154	9	Liaoning	1,558
2	Henan	6,213	10	Shanxi	1,366
3	Shandong	3,931	11	Qinghai	955
4	Xinjiang	3,909	12	Ningxia	844
5	Shaanxi	3,113	13	Tibet	825
6	Hebei	2,995	14	Sichuan	695
7	Gansu	2,003	15	Yunnan	632
8	Heilongjiang	1,595	16	Jilin	369

Cashmere

Tons

| 1 | Inner Mongolia | 79,010 | 9 | Shanxi | 7,872 |
| 2 | Shaanxi | 17,140 | 10 | Heilongjiang | 4,940 |

3	Xinjiang	12,273	11	Ningxia	4,760
4	Liaoning	9,959	12	Qinghai	4,250
5	Tibet	9,230	13	Gansu	4,000
6	Henan	8,870	14	Jilin	1,570
7	Hebei	8,300	15	Sichuan	338
8	Shandong	8,060	16	Beijing	334

Poultry Eggs

Thousand Tons

1	Henan	4,102	9	Heilongjiang	1,027
2	Shandong	3,962	10	Jilin	977
3	Hebei	3,461	11	Hunan	956
4	Liaoning	2,768	12	Shanxi	798
5	Jiangsu	1,979	13	Shaanxi	554
6	Sichuan	1,452	14	Inner Mongolia	551
7	Hubei	1,451	15	Jiangxi	461
8	Anhui	1,245	16	Zhejiang	431

Honey

Thousand Tons

1	Henan	99	9	Jilin	15
2	Zhejiang	80	10	Jiangxi	14
3	Sichuan	45	11	Xinjiang	13
4	Hubei	23	12	Guangxi	12
5	Anhui	20	13	Hebei	12
6	Heilongjiang	18	14	Hunan	12
7	Guangdong	18	15	Fujian	11
8	Chongqing	16	16	Yunnan	7

Biggest Producers of Aquatic Products

Thousand Tons

1	Shandong	8,632	9	Jiangxi	2,426
2	Guangdong	8,161	10	Hunan	2,341
3	Fujian	6,585	11	Anhui	2,155
4	Zhejiang	5,508	12	Hainan	1,831
5	Jiangsu	5,094	13	Sichuan	1,261
6	Liaoning	5,050	14	Hebei	1,231
7	Hubei	4,104	15	Henan	850
8	Guangxi	3,193	16	Heilongjiang	489

Per Capita Output of Major Farm Products

Grain

Kg.

1	Heilongjiang	1,566	9	Jiangxi	469
2	Jilin	1,291	10	Shandong	466
3	Inner Mongolia	1,112	11	Hebei	460
4	Xinjiang	612	12	Gansu	441
5	Henan	607	13	Hunan	439
6	Ningxia	574	14	Hubei	432
7	Anhui	546	15	Jiangsu	432
8	Liaoning	500	16	Sichuan	419

Cottons

Kg.

1	Xinjiang	156.4	9	Gansu	2.7
2	Hubei	7.9	10	Jiangsu	2.6
3	Shandong	6.4	11	Henan	2.0
4	Hebei	6.2	12	Shaanxi	1.5
5	Anhui	4.2	13	Shanxi	0.8

6	Tianjin	3.4	14	Zhejiang	0.5
7	Hunan	3.0	15	Jilin	0.2
8	Jiangxi	2.9	16	Shanghai	0.2

Oil-bearing Crops

Kg.

1	Inner Mongolia	63.4	9	Jilin	30.5
2	Henan	62.6	10	Gansu	27.0
3	Hubei	57.6	11	Xinjiang	27.0
4	Qinghai	56.6	12	Jiangxi	26.4
5	Anhui	37.5	13	Guizhou	26.2
6	Shandong	36.0	14	Liaoning	25.9
7	Sichuan	35.9	15	Ningxia	25.8
8	Hunan	33.7	16	Hebei	20.7

Pork, Beef and Muttons

Kg.

1	Inner Mongolia	85.8	9	Hainan	60.8
2	Tibet	83.9	10	Henan	59.5
3	Sichuan	70.0	11	Guangxi	59.3
4	Hunan	68.9	12	Jiangxi	57.4
5	Yunnan	68.9	13	Chongqing	56.0
6	Jilin	67.5	14	Qinghai	53.4
7	Liaoning	64.9	15	Xinjiang	52.9
8	Hubei	62.0	16	Guizhou	51.9

Total Aquatic Products

Kg.

| 1 | Hainan | 205.6 | 9 | Jiangsu | 64.2 |
| 2 | Fujian | 175.1 | 10 | Jiangxi | 53.8 |

3	Liaoning	115.1	11	Anhui	35.9
4	Zhejiang	100.4	12	Hunan	35.1
5	Shandong	88.9	13	Tianjin	27.6
6	Guangdong	76.9	14	Ningxia	22.3
7	Hubei	70.9	15	Hebei	16.8
8	Guangxi	67.9	16	Sichuan	15.6

Milk

Kg.

1	Inner Mongolia	307.7	9	Shaanxi	37.5
2	Ningxia	160.1	10	Henan	33.6
3	Heilongjiang	135.1	11	Beijing	29.4
4	Tibet	87.0	12	Shandong	28.0
5	Hebei	62.7	13	Liaoning	27.5
6	Xinjiang	60.0	14	Shanxi	23.8
7	Qinghai	47.9	15	Jilin	17.3
8	Tianjin	47.3	16	Gansu	14.9

Industry

Total Assets of Industrial Enterprises

Million Yuan

1	Jiangsu	9,208,169	9	Shanghai	3,353,826
2	Shandong	7,888,106	10	Beijing	3,139,828
3	Guangdong	7,794,352	11	Hubei	3,013,182
4	Zhejiang	5,963,311	12	Shanxi	2,805,827
5	Henan	4,202,192	13	Anhui	2,516,807
6	Liaoning	3,798,929	14	Fujian	2,467,106
7	Hebei	3,604,017	15	Inner Mongolia	2,314,171
8	Sichuan	3,472,916	16	Shaanxi	2,244,311

Revenue from Principal Business of Industrial Enterprises

Million Yuan

1	Shandong	13,231,898	9	Sichuan	3,525,184
2	Jiangsu	13,227,041	10	Shanghai	3,453,353
3	Guangdong	10,365,498	11	Anhui	3,307,946
4	Zhejiang	6,176,548	12	Fujian	3,284,714
5	Henan	5,945,479	13	Hunan	3,161,657
6	Liaoning	5,215,040	14	Tianjin	2,701,112
7	Hebei	4,576,625	15	Jiangxi	2,670,022
8	Hubei	3,786,454	16	Jilin	2,195,072

Total Profits of Industrial Enterprises

Million Yuan

1	Shandong	850,773	9	Sichuan	216,837
2	Jiangsu	783,406	10	Hubei	208,066
3	Guangdong	585,493	11	Tianjin	199,276

4	Henan	441,082	12	Shaanxi	197,332
5	Zhejiang	338,587	13	Fujian	195,945
6	Hebei	256,086	14	Anhui	175,877
7	Liaoning	246,158	15	Jiangxi	175,666
8	Shanghai	241,520	16	Inner Mongolia	168,255

Ratio of Profits, Taxes and Interests to Average Assets of Industrial Enterprises

%

1	Jiangxi	24.38	9	Tianjin	16.09
2	Hunan	21.64	10	Fujian	15.97
3	Shandong	20.21	11	Guangxi	15.70
4	Heilongjiang	19.08	12	Chongqing	15.57
5	Henan	18.49	13	Hubei	15.00
6	Jilin	17.47	14	Yunnan	14.59
7	Shaanxi	16.97	15	Anhui	14.46
8	Jiangsu	16.22	16	Liaoning	14.14

Leading Producers of Industrial Products

Crude Oil

Thousand Tons

1	Heilongjiang	40,010	9	Hebei	5,910
2	Shaanxi	36,880	10	Henan	4,765
3	Tianjin	30,445	11	Qinghai	2,145
4	Xinjiang	27,925	12	Jiangsu	2,015
5	Shandong	27,656	13	Hubei	801
6	Guangdong	12,918	14	Gansu	728
7	Liaoning	10,010	15	Guangxi	437
8	Jilin	6,203	16	Hainan	265

Natural Gas

Million cu. m

1	Shaanxi	37,160	9	Tianjin	1,873
2	Xinjiang	28,291	10	Hebei	1,558
3	Sichuan	21,431	11	Liaoning	760
4	Guangdong	7,526	12	Beijing	579
5	Qinghai	6,806	13	Shandong	511
6	Heilongjiang	3,499	14	Henan	493
7	Shanxi	3,159	15	Hubei	309
8	Jilin	2,370	16	Shanghai	230

Salt

Thousand Tons

1	Shandong	18,417	9	Hunan	2,569
2	Jiangsu	6,989	10	Xinjiang	2,548
3	Sichuan	5,029	11	Inner Mongolia	2,430
4	Hubei	4,650	12	Chongqing	2,363
5	Henan	4,122	13	Anhui	1,561
6	Hebei	3,024	14	Tianjin	1,548
7	Qinghai	2,613	15	Yunnan	1,299
8	Jiangxi	2,573	16	Liaoning	1,250

Refined Sugar

Thousand Tons

1	Guangxi	10,109	9	Hunan	72
2	Yunnan	2,387	10	Liaoning	41
3	Guangdong	1,428	11	Guizhou	39
4	Xinjiang	467	12	Gansu	38
5	Hainan	437	13	Fujian	36
6	Inner Mongolia	423	14	Shandong	36
7	Heilongjiang	172	15	Sichuan	33
8	Hebei	95	16	Jiangxi	32

Beer

Thousand Kiloliter

1	Shandong	6,858	9	Heilongjiang	2,189
2	Guangdong	4,808	10	Fujian	2,000
3	Henan	4,279	11	Guangxi	1,851
4	Zhejiang	2,894	12	Beijing	1,683
5	Liaoning	2,720	13	Anhui	1,636
6	Hubei	2,547	14	Hebei	1,566
7	Sichuan	2,383	15	Jilin	1,486
8	Jiangsu	2,200	16	Jiangxi	1,244

Cigarettes

Million Pieces

1	Yunnan	378,780	9	Jiangsu	102,130
2	Hunan	186,210	10	Sichuan	99,870
3	Henan	171,300	11	Fujian	94,860
4	Shandong	142,010	12	Shanghai	93,420
5	Hubei	139,800	13	Zhejiang	92,350
6	Guangdong	139,190	14	Shaanxi	89,950
7	Anhui	131,340	15	Hebei	84,750
8	Guizhou	127,140	16	Guangxi	76,850

Cloth

Million Meter

1	Zhejiang	24,499	9	Sichuan	1,784
2	Shandong	14,335	10	Anhui	1,091
3	Jiangsu	13,223	11	Jiangxi	808
4	Hubei	8,296	12	Shaanxi	738
5	Hebei	7,245	13	Chongqing	704
6	Fujian	6,572	14	Liaoning	413
7	Henan	3,891	15	Hunan	384
8	Guangdong	3,630	16	Tianjin	210

Machine-made Paper and Paperboards

Thousand Tons

1	Shandong	20,135	9	Guangxi	3,717
2	Guangdong	18,703	10	Chongqing	2,521
3	Zhejiang	16,231	11	Tianjin	2,311
4	Jiangsu	12,078	12	Anhui	2,218
5	Henan	8,261	13	Sichuan	2,123
6	Fujian	6,113	14	Hubei	2,103
7	Hebei	4,859	15	Jiangxi	1,813
8	Hunan	4,068	16	Hainan	1,455

Coke

Thousand Tons

1	Shanxi	90,768	9	Xinjiang	20,108
2	Hebei	63,958	10	Yunnan	17,367
3	Shandong	43,172	11	Sichuan	14,531
4	Shaanxi	34,439	12	Hubei	9,434
5	Inner Mongolia	31,149	13	Anhui	9,044
6	Henan	27,067	14	Guizhou	8,749
7	Jiangsu	22,525	15	Jiangxi	8,260
8	Liaoning	21,471	16	Heilongjiang	8,152

Sulfuric Acid

Thousand Tons

1	Yunnan	13,367	9	Jiangxi	3,235
2	Hubei	6,801	10	Hunan	3,108
3	Shandong	6,580	11	Guangdong	2,829
4	Guizhou	6,342	12	Guangxi	2,817
5	Sichuan	6,041	13	Inner Mongolia	2,777
6	Anhui	5,909	14	Gansu	2,760
7	Henan	3,800	15	Chongqing	2,094
8	Jiangsu	3,714	16	Hebei	1,612

Caustic Soda

Thousand Tons

1	Shandong	5,813	9	Hebei	1,016
2	Jiangsu	4,136	10	Hubei	992
3	Xinjiang	2,134	11	Hunan	750
4	Inner Mongolia	1,968	12	Shanghai	712
5	Henan	1,814	13	Shaanxi	678
6	Zhejiang	1,457	14	Liaoning	564
7	Tianjin	1,124	15	Jiangxi	526
8	Sichuan	1,116	16	Shanxi	495

Soda Ash

Thousand Tons

1	Shandong	3,946	9	Hunan	607
2	Henan	3,379	10	Guangdong	607
3	Jiangsu	3,255	11	Inner Mongolia	599
4	Hebei	2,571	12	Anhui	547
5	Qinghai	2,282	13	Tianjin	531
6	Sichuan	1,808	14	Liaoning	468
7	Hubei	1,322	15	Shaanxi	381
8	Chongqing	1,187	16	Zhejiang	268

Ethylene

Thousand Tons

1	Guangdong	2,383	9	Heilongjiang	760
2	Shanghai	2,120	10	Jilin	734
3	Jiangsu	1,459	11	Beijing	723
4	Xinjiang	1,319	12	Fujian	714
5	Tianjin	1,308	13	Gansu	632
6	Liaoning	1,285	14	Hubei	565
7	Zhejiang	1,140	15	Henan	301
8	Shandong	783			

Chemical Fertilizer

Thousand Tons

1	Hubei	11,569	9	Yunnan	3,419
2	Shandong	7,600	10	Anhui	2,773
3	Guizhou	5,336	11	Jiangsu	2,508
4	Henan	4,886	12	Hebei	2,184
5	Sichuan	4,737	13	Chongqing	2,154
6	Shanxi	4,461	14	Hunan	1,355
7	Qinghai	4,252	15	Inner Mongolia	1,136
8	Xinjiang	3,618	16	Jiangxi	1,073

Chemical Pesticide

Thousand Tons

1	Shandong	906	9	Inner Mongolia	75
2	Jiangsu	757	10	Jiangxi	42
3	Zhejiang	291	11	Ningxia	36
4	Hubei	272	12	Hebei	27
5	Henan	216	13	Guangdong	23
6	Anhui	198	14	Shaanxi	17
7	Sichuan	150	15	Liaoning	14
8	Hunan	116	16	Heilongjiang	11

Primary Plastic

Thousand Tons

1	Jiangsu	8,322	9	Henan	2,096
2	Guangdong	5,855	10	Liaoning	2,080
3	Zhejiang	5,841	11	Fujian	1,649
4	Xinjiang	5,073	12	Heilongjiang	1,401
5	Shandong	4,622	13	Sichuan	1,171
6	Tianjin	3,429	14	Gansu	1,161
7	Shanghai	3,355	15	Shaanxi	1,159
8	Inner Mongolia	3,354	16	Beijing	1,021

Chemical Fiber

Thousand Tons

1	Zhejiang	18,393	9	Hebei	522
2	Jiangsu	12,963	10	Shanghai	478
3	Fujian	3,767	11	Jiangxi	420
4	Sichuan	915	12	Anhui	327
5	Shandong	717	13	Jilin	274
6	Guangdong	560	14	Hubei	217
7	Xinjiang	559	15	Liaoning	174
8	Henan	538	16	Tianjin	122

Cement

Thousand Tons

1	Jiangsu	180,271	9	Hunan	113,141
2	Henan	167,820	10	Hubei	110,494
3	Shandong	162,387	11	Guangxi	109,084
4	Sichuan	139,472	12	Jiangxi	92,281
5	Guangdong	134,294	13	Yunnan	91,218
6	Hebei	127,474	14	Shaanxi	86,038
7	Zhejiang	124,796	15	Guizhou	81,892
8	Anhui	121,919	16	Fujian	79,058

Plate Glass

Thousand Weight Cases

1	Hebei	118,364	9	Anhui	33,468
2	Guangdong	85,866	10	Liaoning	30,157
3	Shandong	82,797	11	Tianjin	21,371
4	Hubei	81,328	12	Shanxi	20,653
5	Jiangsu	59,306	13	Shaanxi	18,379
6	Fujian	52,432	14	Hunan	18,327
7	Sichuan	40,075	15	Chongqing	12,502
8	Zhejiang	35,912	16	Henan	11,280

Pig Iron

Thousand Tons

1	Hebei	170,276	9	Anhui	20,173
2	Jiangsu	66,906	10	Jiangxi	20,122
3	Shandong	65,803	11	Sichuan	20,114
4	Liaoning	56,980	12	Yunnan	19,365
5	Shanxi	43,032	13	Hunan	17,398
6	Henan	25,519	14	Shanghai	16,376
7	Hubei	24,162	15	Guangxi	15,676
8	Tianjin	22,142	16	Xinjiang	13,707

Rolled Steel

Thousand Tons

1	Hebei	228,616	9	Guangdong	33,845
2	Jiangsu	123,980	10	Hubei	33,449
3	Shandong	81,091	11	Anhui	31,386
4	Liaoning	68,630	12	Guangxi	27,907
5	Tianjin	66,409	13	Sichuan	27,852
6	Shanxi	44,862	14	Fujian	27,828
7	Henan	42,552	15	Jiangxi	24,638
8	Zhejiang	38,234	16	Shanghai	23,228

Motor Vehicles

Thousand Units

1	Shanghai	2,269	9	Jiangsu	1,072
2	Beijing	2,000	10	Shandong	1,044
3	Guangdong	1,999	11	Anhui	1,007
4	Guangxi	1,869	12	Hebei	974
5	Chongqing	1,840	13	Sichuan	805
6	Jilin	1,647	14	Tianjin	557
7	Hubei	1,587	15	Shaanxi	422
8	Liaoning	1,080	16	Henan	406

Power Generation Equipment

Thousand Km

1	Sichuan	38,846	9	Guangdong	3,845
2	Shanghai	25,388	10	Chongqing	2,880
3	Heilongjiang	19,065	11	Hubei	1,457
4	Shandong	9,397	12	Hunan	1,359
5	Beijing	5,081	13	Fujian	1,037
6	Zhejiang	5,008	14	Henan	983
7	Jiangsu	4,224	15	Yunnan	772
8	Xinjiang	3,888	16	Inner Mongolia	584

Household Refrigerators

Thousand Units

1	Anhui	29,739	9	Guizhou	1,553
2	Guangdong	19,460	10	Shanghai	1,539
3	Jiangsu	10,631	11	Jiangxi	1,015
4	Zhejiang	9,396	12	Sichuan	897
5	Shandong	5,244	13	Liaoning	848
6	Henan	5,178	14	Beijing	837
7	Chongqing	3,200	15	Tianjin	493
8	Hubei	2,261	16	Hunan	210

Air Conditioners

Thousand Units

1	Guangdong	48,686	9	Jiangxi	3,199
2	Anhui	27,124	10	Jiangsu	2,709
3	Hubei	11,894	11	Tianjin	2,182
4	Chongqing	9,850	12	Sichuan	1,397
5	Shandong	6,372	13	Liaoning	1,066
6	Hebei	6,330	14	Henan	13
7	Zhejiang	5,650			
8	Shanghai	4,100			

Household Washing Machines

Thousand Units

1	Zhejiang	18,814	9	Hubei	1,376
2	Anhui	16,978	10	Henan	832
3	Jiangsu	13,544	11	Jiangxi	464
4	Guangdong	6,652	12	Hunan	372
5	Shandong	6,514	13	Tianjin	260
6	Chongqing	2,419	14	Gansu	41
7	Sichuan	1,911			
8	Shanghai	1,842			

Mobile Telephones

Thousand Units

1	Guangdong	736,723	9	Chongqing	35,457
2	Beijing	187,167	10	Jiangsu	30,196
3	Tianjin	103,363	11	Liaoning	27,150
4	Henan	97,207	12	Shanxi	23,876
5	Jiangxi	55,134	13	Zhejiang	9,878
6	Shandong	50,967	14	Sichuan	8,144
7	Shanghai	43,849	15	Hubei	7,148
8	Fujian	38,418	16	Hunan	875

Computer Equipment

Thousand Units

1	Shanghai	81,013	9	Anhui	6,718
2	Jiangsu	75,207	10	Zhejiang	1,643
3	Sichuan	59,162	11	Hubei	979
4	Chongqing	55,935	12	Hunan	347
5	Guangdong	20,287	13	Shandong	224
6	Fujian	12,848	14	Jiangxi	77
7	Beijing	11,411	15	Heilongjiang	35
8	Tianjin	10,722	16	Liaoning	2

Color Television Sets

Thousand Units

1	Guangdong	63,646	9	Tianjin	2,771
2	Shandong	14,697	10	Inner Mongolia	1,809
3	Fujian	8,913	11	Guizhou	1,220
4	Jiangsu	8,844	12	Beijing	1,000
5	Sichuan	7,952	13	Shanghai	994
6	Zhejiang	6,286	14	Guangxi	772
7	Liaoning	4,406	15	Jiangxi	468
8	Anhui	3,205	16	Henan	464

Electricity

Million Kwh.

1	Jiangsu	428,941	9	Hebei	249,937
2	Guangdong	396,480	10	Hubei	215,822
3	Inner Mongolia	352,070	11	Yunnan	214,842
4	Shandong	351,094	12	Anhui	196,576
5	Zhejiang	293,930	13	Fujian	176,766
6	Henan	286,177	14	Guizhou	167,628
7	Shanxi	262,792	15	Xinjiang	161,169
8	Sichuan	259,733	16	Liaoning	154,433

Total Output Value of Construction

Million Yuan

1	Jiangsu	2,171,216	9	Henan	708,237
2	Zhejiang	2,006,642	10	Fujian	545,941
3	Liaoning	874,337	11	Hunan	525,598
4	Hubei	834,340	12	Hebei	520,392
5	Shandong	833,270	13	Shanghai	510,284
6	Guangdong	772,924	14	Anhui	497,034
7	Beijing	740,709	15	Chongqing	473,188
8	Sichuan	723,949	16	Shaanxi	399,381

Business

Investment Completed for Enterprises such as Real Estate

Million Yuan

1	Jiangsu	724,145	9	Fujian	370,297
2	Guangdong	648,959	10	Beijing	348,340
3	Liaoning	645,075	11	Hebei	344,542
4	Zhejiang	621,625	12	Hubei	328,602
5	Shandong	544,453	13	Chongqing	301,278
6	Anhui	394,623	14	Shanghai	281,959
7	Sichuan	385,300	15	Hunan	262,832
8	Henan	384,376	16	Yunnan	248,833

Average Selling Price of Commercialized Buildings

Yuan/sq. m

1	Beijing	18,553	9	Chongqing	5,569
2	Shanghai	16,420	10	Sichuan	5,498
3	Zhejiang	11,042	11	Shaanxi	5,280
4	Guangdong	9,090	12	Hubei	5,266
5	Fujian	9,050	13	Jiangxi	5,203
6	Tianjin	8,746	14	Liaoning	5,122
7	Hainan	8,669	15	Anhui	5,080
8	Jiangsu	6,909	16	Shandong	5,049

Total Retail Sales of Consumer Goods

Million Yuan

1	Guangdong	2,545,393	9	Hebei	1,051,675
2	Shandong	2,229,484	10	Hunan	901,864
3	Jiangsu	2,079,652	11	Beijing	837,510

4	Zhejiang	1,522,554	12	Fujian	827,535
5	Henan	1,242,660	13	Shanghai	805,196
6	Hubei	1,088,594	14	Anhui	654,242
7	Liaoning	1,058,144	15	Heilongjiang	625,117
8	Sichuan	1,056,145	16	Jilin	542,643

Business Revenue of Hotels

Million Yuan

1	Guangdong	48,050	9	Henan	14,187
2	Beijing	35,281	10	Sichuan	13,878
3	Zhejiang	27,594	11	Hubei	12,363
4	Shanghai	25,136	12	Liaoning	10,687
5	Shandong	21,770	13	Shaanxi	10,157
6	Jiangsu	21,159	14	Hainan	9,400
7	Hunan	14,923	15	Yunnan	8,407
8	Fujian	14,728	16	Hebei	7,494

Business Revenue of Catering Services

Million Yuan

1	Guangdong	60,406	9	Chongqing	16,298
2	Beijing	52,072	10	Fujian	15,890
3	Shanghai	46,948	11	Henan	15,045
4	Jiangsu	39,954	12	Liaoning	14,272
5	Shandong	33,588	13	Shaanxi	12,561
6	Zhejiang	26,099	14	Hunan	10,929
7	Sichuan	23,134	15	Tianjin	10,362
8	Hubei	22,579	16	Anhui	10,008

Biggest Traders of Goods

Million Dollar

#	Province	Value	#	Province	Value
1	Guangdong	1,281,192	9	Liaoning	121,361
2	Jiangsu	593,295	10	Hebei	90,219
3	Shanghai	434,278	11	Henan	62,774
4	Zhejiang	365,508	12	Chongqing	58,785
5	Shandong	314,942	13	Sichuan	55,095
6	Fujian	154,483	14	Anhui	38,928
7	Tianjin	134,600	15	Guangxi	38,696
8	Beijing	131,561	16	Xinjiang	37,568

% of China

#	Province	%	#	Province	%
1	Guangdong	30.8	9	Liaoning	2.9
2	Jiangsu	14.3	10	Hebei	2.2
3	Shanghai	10.4	11	Henan	1.5
4	Zhejiang	8.8	12	Chongqing	1.4
5	Shandong	7.6	13	Sichuan	1.3
6	Fujian	3.7	14	Anhui	0.9
7	Tianjin	3.2	15	Guangxi	0.9
8	Beijing	3.2	16	Xinjiang	0.9

Biggest Exporters

% of Total China Exports

#	Province	%	#	Province	%
1	Guangdong	33.1	9	Hebei	1.8
2	Jiangsu	15.1	10	Henan	1.7
3	Zhejiang	11.9	11	Chongqing	1.7
4	Shanghai	8.5	12	Beijing	1.5
5	Shandong	6.4	13	Sichuan	1.5
6	Fujian	4.3	14	Jiangxi	1.1
7	Liaoning	2.4	15	Anhui	1.0
8	Tianjin	2.2	16	Hubei	1.0

Biggest Importers

% of Total China Imports

National Total	100.0			
1 Guangdong	28.2	9	Fujian	3.1
2 Jiangsu	13.3	10	Hebei	2.5
3 Shanghai	12.6	11	Guangxi	1.5
4 Shandong	8.9	12	Henan	1.2
5 Zhejiang	5.3	13	Sichuan	1.1
6 Beijing	5.0	14	Xinjiang	1.1
7 Tianjin	4.4	15	Chongqing	1.1
8 Liaoning	3.5	16	Jilin	1.0

Transport

Longest Railways Networks

Km

			Km				Km
	National Total	103144.6					
1	Inner Mongolia	10203.3		9	Shandong	4288.1
2	Hebei	6255.5		10	Hunan	4026.6
3	Heilongjiang	6021.8		11	Guangxi	4013.4
4	Liaoning	5104.4		12	Hubei	3929.5
5	Henan	4890.4		13	Shanxi	3786.4
6	Xinjiang	4741.3		14	Sichuan	3539.4
7	Shaanxi	4421.1		15	Anhui	3513.1
8	Jilin	4397.2		16	Guangdong	3471.7

Longest Navigable Inland Waterways

Km

1	Jiangsu	24,333	9	Guangxi	5,478
2	Guangdong	12,097	10	Heilongjiang	5,098
3	Hunan	11,496	11	Chongqing	4,331
4	Sichuan	10,720	12	Guizhou	3,649
5	Zhejiang	9,743	13	Yunnan	3,551
6	Hubei	8,271	14	Fujian	3,245
7	Anhui	5,642	15	Inner Mongolia	2,403
8	Jiangxi	5,638	16	Shanghai	2,268

Longest Highways

Km

1	Sichuan	301,816	9	Anhui	173,763
2	Shandong	252,786	10	Guizhou	172,564
3	Henan	249,831	11	Xinjiang	170,155

4	Hunan	235,392	12	Inner Mongolia	167,515
5	Hubei	226,912	13	Shaanxi	165,249
6	Yunnan	222,940	14	Heilongjiang	160,206
7	Guangdong	202,915	15	Jiangsu	156,094
8	Hebei	174,492	16	Jiangxi	152,067

Most Crowded Road Networks

Number of Vehicles Per Km of Road Network

National Total   29.1

1	Beijing	238.6	9	Liaoning	41
2	Shanghai	186.0	10	Fujian	33
3	Tianjin	166.4	11	Henan	28
4	Zhejiang	78.1	12	Ningxia	28
5	Jiangsu	60.5	13	Shanxi	27
6	Guangdong	58.0	14	Jilin	26
7	Shandong	47.5	15	Hainan	26
8	Hebei	46.8	16	Guangxi	25

Passenger Traffic

Thousand Persons

1	Hunan	1,597,259	9	Hubei	915,225
2	Guangdong	1,531,204	10	Guizhou	834,358
3	Jiangsu	1,514,441	11	Shandong	750,743
4	Henan	1,362,373	12	Shaanxi	701,333
5	Zhejiang	1,353,483	13	Chongqing	651,834
6	Sichuan	1,347,747	14	Jiangxi	650,668
7	Anhui	1,267,105	15	Beijing	641,606
8	Liaoning	917,353	16	Hebei	617,179

Passenger Traffic by Railways

Thousand Persons

1	Guangdong	176,584	9	Shandong	92,463
2	Jiangsu	134,351	10	Hunan	92,309
3	Liaoning	130,333	11	Hebei	87,619
4	Beijing	116,796	12	Sichuan	82,397
5	Zhejiang	110,523	13	Shanghai	79,715
6	Henan	105,323	14	Anhui	72,105
7	Hubei	104,105	15	Jiangxi	69,448
8	Heilongjiang	101,069	16	Jilin	66,288

Passenger Traffic by Highways

Thousand Persons

1	Hunan	1,490,150	9	Liaoning	781,680
2	Jiangsu	1,355,550	10	Guizhou	773,590
3	Guangdong	1,333,050	11	Shandong	640,190
4	Henan	1,254,500	12	Shaanxi	636,500
5	Sichuan	1,241,450	13	Chongqing	612,430
6	Zhejiang	1,211,850	14	Jiangxi	579,150
7	Anhui	1,194,330	15	Hebei	529,560
8	Hubei	806,700	16	Beijing	524,810

Passenger Traffic by Waterways

Thousand Persons

1	Zhejiang	31,110	9	Hainan	13,560
2	Jiangsu	24,540	10	Yunnan	10,450
3	Sichuan	23,900	11	Chongqing	6,890
4	Guangdong	21,570	12	Liaoning	5,340
5	Shandong	18,090	13	Hubei	4,420
6	Guizhou	17,550	14	Guangxi	3,940

| 7 | Fujian | 17,110 | 15 | Shaanxi | 3,600 |
| 8 | Hunan | 14,800 | 16 | Heilongjiang | 3,570 |

Cargo Handled

Thousand Tons

1	Anhui	3,963,910	9	Jiangsu	1,817,754
2	Guangdong	3,490,110	10	Sichuan	1,677,591
3	Shandong	2,641,002	11	Inner Mongolia	1,643,461
4	Liaoning	2,068,680	12	Shanxi	1,560,455
5	Hebei	1,980,091	13	Guangxi	1,511,432
6	Zhejiang	1,886,791	14	Shaanxi	1,415,789
7	Henan	1,848,228	15	Jiangxi	1,351,719
8	Hunan	1,845,351	16	Hubei	1,310,001

Highest Car Ownership

Number of Per 1,000 Population

National Total   77.2

1	Beijing	200.9	9	Guangdong	93.6
2	Tianjin	152.4	10	Shanxi	87.8
3	Zhejiang	138.9	11	Liaoning	81.1
4	Shandong	106.8	12	Qinghai	77.3
5	Inner Mongolia	105.6	13	Xinjiang	75.6
6	Ningxia	99.9	14	Jilin	74.9
7	Jiangsu	98.3	15	Shaanxi	74.6
8	Hebei	98.1	16	Fujian	73.5

Cars Sold

New Car Registrations, '000
National Total   20,309

1	Shandong	1,838	9	Hunan	686
2	Guangdong	1,612	10	Hubei	643
3	Jiangsu	1,568	11	Liaoning	634
4	Zhejiang	1,409	12	Yunnan	610
5	Hebei	1,385	13	Shaanxi	595
6	Henan	1,265	14	Shanxi	591
7	Sichuan	962	15	Beijing	589
8	Anhui	693	16	Fujian	557

Research and Innovation

Full-time Equivalent of R&D Personnel of Industrial Enterprises

Man-year

1	Guangdong	426,330	9	Hubei	85,826
2	Jiangsu	393,942	10	Hunan	73,558
3	Zhejiang	263,507	11	Tianjin	68,175
4	Shandong	227,403	12	Hebei	65,049
5	Henan	125,091	13	Liaoning	59,090
6	Fujian	100,200	14	Sichuan	58,148
7	Shanghai	92,136	15	Beijing	58,036
8	Anhui	86,000	16	Shaanxi	45,809

Expenditure on R&D of Industrial Enterprises

Thousand Yuan

1	Jiangsu	123,957,454	9	Henan	29,534,095
2	Guangdong	123,747,912	10	Fujian	27,919,658
3	Shandong	105,280,967	11	Hunan	27,039,872
4	Zhejiang	68,435,620	12	Anhui	24,772,461
5	Shanghai	40,478,002	13	Hebei	23,274,183
6	Liaoning	33,313,026	14	Beijing	21,306,175
7	Hubei	31,179,866	15	Sichuan	16,889,023
8	Tianjin	30,003,772	16	Shaanxi	14,014,799

Patent Applications Granted

Piece

1	Jiangsu	239,645	9	Fujian	37,511
2	Zhejiang	202,350	10	Henan	29,482
3	Guangdong	170,430	11	Hubei	28,760

4	Shandong	76,976	12	Tianjin	24,856
5	Beijing	62,671	13	Chongqing	24,828
6	Anhui	48,849	14	Hunan	24,392
7	Shanghai	48,680	15	Liaoning	21,656
8	Sichuan	46,171	16	Shaanxi	20,836

Patent Applications Granted

No. of Patents Granted Per 100,000 People

1	Zhejiang	368.0	9	Anhui	81.0
2	Jiangsu	301.8	10	Shandong	79.1
3	Beijing	296.3	11	Sichuan	57.0
4	Shanghai	201.6	12	Shaanxi	55.4
5	Tianjin	168.8	13	Heilongjiang	51.7
6	Guangdong	160.1	14	Hubei	49.6
7	Fujian	99.4	15	Liaoning	49.3
8	Chongqing	83.6	16	Hunan	36.5

Public Finance

Largest Government Revenue

Billion Yuan

1	Guangdong	708.1		9	Henan	241.5
2	Jiangsu	656.8		10	Hebei	229.6
3	Shandong	456.0		11	Hubei	219.1
4	Shanghai	411.0		12	Fujian	211.9
5	Zhejiang	379.7		13	Tianjin	207.9
6	Beijing	366.1		14	Anhui	207.5
7	Liaoning	334.4		15	Hunan	203.1
8	Sichuan	278.4		16	Shaanxi	174.8

Government Revenue

As % of GDP

1	Shanghai	19.0		9	Chongqing	13.4
2	Beijing	18.8		10	Liaoning	12.3
3	Hainan	15.3		11	Ningxia	12.0
4	Guizhou	15.1		12	Tibet	11.8
5	Tianjin	14.5		13	Guangdong	11.4
6	Yunnan	13.7		14	Jiangxi	11.3
7	Shanxi	13.5		15	Jiangsu	11.1
8	Xinjiang	13.5		16	Anhui	10.9

Government Spending

As % of GDP

1	Tibet	125.6		9	Jiangxi	24.2
2	Qinghai	58.4		10	Chongqing	24.2
3	Guizhou	38.5		11	Shanxi	24.0
4	Gansu	36.8		12	Sichuan	23.7

5	Xinjiang	36.7	13	Heilongjiang	23.4
6	Ningxia	36.0	14	Anhui	22.8
7	Yunnan	35.0	15	Shaanxi	22.8
8	Hainan	32.1	16	Guangxi	22.3

Tax Revenue

As % of GDP

1	Beijing	18.0	9	Guangdong	9.3
2	Shanghai	17.6	10	Ningxia	9.3
3	Hainan	13.1	11	Jiangsu	9.2
4	Guizhou	10.5	12	Tianjin	9.1
5	Yunnan	10.4	13	Shanxi	9.0
6	Xinjiang	9.9	14	Tibet	8.9
7	Zhejiang	9.4	15	Chongqing	8.8
8	Liaoning	9.3	16	Qinghai	8.3

Inflation

Highest Consumer Price Index

Preceding Year = 100

	National	102.6			
1	Qinghai	103.9	9	Tianjin	103.1
2	Xinjiang	103.9	10	Shanxi	103.1
3	Tibet	103.6	11	Shaanxi	103.0
4	Ningxia	103.4	12	Hebei	103.0
5	Beijing	103.3	13	Jilin	102.9
6	Inner Mongolia	103.2	14	Henan	102.9
7	Gansu	103.2	15	Hubei	102.8
8	Yunnan	103.1	16	Sichuan	102.8

Highest Retail Price Index

Preceding Year = 100

	National	101.4			
1	Xinjiang	103.3	9	Henan	101.9
2	Tibet	103.0	10	Shanxi	101.8
3	Qinghai	102.7	11	Hubei	101.8
4	Inner Mongolia	102.6	12	Shaanxi	101.8
5	Yunnan	102.6	13	Chongqing	101.8
6	Gansu	102.6	14	Hunan	101.7
7	Ningxia	102.4	15	Tianjin	101.7
8	Hebei	102.2	16	Sichuan	101.7

Education

Most Students Per 100,000 Population

Pre-education

Number

1	Guangxi	3,881	9	Xinjiang	3,220
2	Fujian	3,823	10	Guizhou	3,093
3	Henan	3,689	11	Chongqing	3,033
4	Jiangxi	3,471	12	Jiangsu	2,927
5	Zhejiang	3,412	13	Hebei	2,922
6	Shaanxi	3,387	14	Qinghai	2,909
7	Hainan	3,368	15	Hunan	2,880
8	Guangdong	3,347	16	Sichuan	2,866

Primary Education

Number

1	Guizhou	10,205	9	Hainan	8,345
2	Henan	9,993	10	Qinghai	8,283
3	Tibet	9,571	11	Guangdong	7,626
4	Ningxia	9,335	12	Hebei	7,495
5	Guangxi	9,104	13	Gansu	7,243
6	Jiangxi	9,061	14	Hunan	7,046
7	Xinjiang	8,484	15	Fujian	6,933
8	Yunnan	8,416	16	Anhui	6,834

Junior Secondary

Number

1	Guizhou	6,036	9	Hainan	3,910
2	Ningxia	4,401	10	Jiangxi	3,895
3	Guangxi	4,167	11	Guangdong	3,821

4	Xinjiang	4,113	12	Qinghai	3,632
5	Tibet	4,095	13	Shanxi	3,576
6	Henan	4,094	14	Chongqing	3,455
7	Yunnan	4,023	15	Sichuan	3,365
8	Gansu	4,018	16	Anhui	3,335

Senior Secondary

Number

1	Guangdong	4,239	9	Anhui	3,794
2	Ningxia	4,097	10	Guangxi	3,727
3	Gansu	4,048	11	Qinghai	3,638
4	Shaanxi	4,012	12	Henan	3,571
5	Chongqing	3,989	13	Sichuan	3,497
6	Guizhou	3,943	14	Fujian	3,341
7	Shanxi	3,872	15	Jiangxi	3,336
8	Hainan	3,846	16	Xinjiang	3,266

Higher Education

Number

1	Beijing	5,469	9	Jiangsu	2,814
2	Tianjin	4,346	10	Heilongjiang	2,529
3	Shaanxi	3,612	11	Shanxi	2,474
4	Shanghai	3,421	12	Fujian	2,435
5	Hubei	3,144	13	Jiangxi	2,381
6	Jilin	3,033	14	Zhejiang	2,363
7	Liaoning	2,903	15	Shandong	2,304
8	Chongqing	2,894	16	Hainan	2,253

Health

Most Medical Technical Personnel
Per 1,000 Pop.

Number

#		Number	#		Number
1	Beijing	15.46	9	Liaoning	6.01
2	Shanghai	10.97	10	Inner Mongolia	6.01
3	Tianjin	8.05	11	Shanxi	5.77
4	Zhejiang	7.30	12	Qinghai	5.66
5	Xinjiang	6.43	13	Jiangsu	5.63
6	Guangdong	6.32	14	Ningxia	5.58
7	Shandong	6.21	15	Heilongjiang	5.49
8	Shaanxi	6.04	16	Jilin	5.45

Most Licensed (Assistant) Doctors
Per 1,000 Pop.

Number

#		Number	#		Number
1	Beijing	5.85	9	Guangdong	2.40
2	Shanghai	4.05	10	Xinjiang	2.34
3	Tianjin	3.18	11	Jilin	2.31
4	Zhejiang	2.86	12	Qinghai	2.31
5	Inner Mongolia	2.52	13	Jiangsu	2.23
6	Shanxi	2.50	14	Ningxia	2.14
7	Liaoning	2.44	15	Heilongjiang	2.13
8	Shandong	2.41	16	Hebei	2.00

Most Hospital Beds

Beds Per 1,000 pop.

1	Xinjiang	6.06	9	Shaanxi	4.92
2	Liaoning	5.51	10	Beijing	4.92
3	Sichuan	5.26	11	Jilin	4.84
4	Qinghai	5.11	12	Inner Mongolia	4.81
5	Shandong	5.03	13	Guizhou	4.76
6	Hubei	4.97	14	Ningxia	4.76
7	Chongqing	4.96	15	Shanxi	4.76
8	Heilongjiang	4.93	16	Shanghai	4.73

Marriage and Divorce

Highest Marriage Rate

Number of Marriages Per 1,000 Population

1	Henan	13.4	9	Fujian	10.5
2	Anhui	13.4	10	Chongqing	10.2
3	Guizhou	12.3	11	Hainan	10.2
4	Xinjiang	11.5	12	Hebei	10.1
5	Jiangsu	11.4	13	Guangxi	10.0
6	Hubei	11.1	14	Heilongjiang	9.8
7	Shanxi	10.6	15	Ningxia	9.8
8	Shaanxi	10.5	16	Yunnan	9.6

Highest Divorce Rate

Number of Divorces Per 1,000 Population

1	Xinjiang	4.8	9	Beijing	3.1
2	Heilongjiang	4.7	10	Shanghai	2.9
3	Jilin	4.5	11	Jiangsu	2.7
4	Chongqing	4.5	12	Hubei	2.6
5	Liaoning	3.5	13	Anhui	2.6
6	Sichuan	3.3	14	Hunan	2.5
7	Inner Mongolia	3.2	15	Guizhou	2.5
8	Tianjin	3.1	16	Hebei	2.4

Resource and Environment

Ensured Reserves of Petroleum

Thousand Tons

National Total   3,367,328

#	Province	Reserves	#	Province	Reserves
1	Xinjiang	583,936	9	Liaoning	164,112
2	Ocean	498,498	10	Inner Mongolia	83,394
3	Heilongjiang	473,113	11	Qinghai	62,849
4	Shandong	338,394	12	Henan	50,374
5	Shaanxi	337,126	13	Tianjin	31,152
6	Hebei	266,853	14	Jiangsu	30,234
7	Gansu	211,500	15	Ningxia	23,140
8	Jilin	183,266	16	Hubei	13,037

Ensured Reserves of Natural Gas

Million cu. m

National Total   4,642,884

#	Province	Reserves	#	Province	Reserves
1	Sichuan	1,187,438	9	Jilin	75,635
2	Xinjiang	905,388	10	Shandong	35,790
3	Inner Mongolia	804,254	11	Hebei	32,586
4	Shaanxi	623,114	12	Ningxia	29,440
5	Ocean	331,233	13	Tianjin	27,979
6	Chongqing	247,283	14	Gansu	24,128
7	Qinghai	151,179	15	Liaoning	16,946
8	Heilongjiang	135,393	16	Henan	7,209

Ensured Reserves of Coal

Million Tons

National Total   236,290

#	Province	Reserves	#	Province	Reserves
1	Shanxi	90,680	9	Heilongjiang	6,138
2	Inner Mongolia	46,010	10	Yunnan	6,010

3	Xinjiang	15,653	11	Sichuan	5,574
4	Shaanxi	10,438	12	Hebei	3,941
5	Henan	8,955	13	Ningxia	3,847
6	Anhui	8,519	14	Gansu	3,269
7	Guizhou	8,329	15	Liaoning	2,833
8	Shandong	7,878	16	Chongqing	1,986

Ensured Reserves of Iron

Ore, Million Tons

National Total   19,917

1	Liaoning	5,625	9	Xinjiang	456
2	Sichuan	2,660	10	Jilin	452
3	Hebei	2,397	11	Yunnan	413
4	Inner Mongolia	2,099	12	Shaanxi	399
5	Shanxi	1,270	13	Gansu	371
6	Shandong	937	14	Fujian	324
7	Anhui	790	15	Hunan	179
8	Hubei	605	16	Jiangsu	176

Ensured Reserves of Manganese

Ore, Thousand Tons

National Total   215,477

1	Guangxi	84,415	9	Xinjiang	5,672
2	Guizhou	42,478	10	Shaanxi	2,773
3	Hunan	19,084	11	Gansu	2,590
4	Chongqing	17,126	12	Fujian	1,351
5	Liaoning	14,029	13	Sichuan	1,000
6	Yunnan	10,748	14	Guangdong	752
7	Hubei	7,496	15	Shanxi	129
8	Inner Mongolia	5,677	16	Anhui	74

Ensured Reserves of Chromite

Ore, Thousand Tons

National Total		4,015			
1	Tibet	1,692	4	Xinjiang	440
2	Gansu	1,236	5	Hebei	46
3	Inner Mongolia	563	6	Qinghai	37

Ensured Reserves of Titanium

Thousand Tons

National Total		219,570			
1	Sichuan	198,872	4	Hebei	2,837
2	Hubei	10,532	5	Xinjiang	457
3	Shandong	6,867	6	Henan	5

Ensured Reserves of Vanadium

Thousand Tons

National Total		9,099.1			
1	Sichuan	5,761.9	8	Anhui	59.8
2	Guangxi	1,714.9	9	Jiangsu	46.8
3	Gansu	898.7	10	Zhejiang	37.6
4	Hubei	293.7	11	Hunan	29.0
5	Hebei	102.8	12	Inner Mongolia	7.7
6	Shaanxi	78.7	13	Xinjiang	1.6
7	Jiangxi	65.2	14	Yunnan	0.7

Ensured Reserves of Copper

Metal, Thousand Tons

National Total		27,515			
1	Jiangxi	5,971	9	Heilongjiang	1,106
2	Inner Mongolia	4,003	10	Hubei	966

3	Yunnan	2,969	11	Fujian	878
4	Tibet	2,744	12	Sichuan	544
5	Xinjiang	1,682	13	Guangdong	306
6	Anhui	1,681	14	Liaoning	302
7	Shanxi	1,582	15	Qinghai	256
8	Gansu	1,527	16	Jilin	197

Ensured Reserves of Lead

Metal, Thousand Tons

National Total		15,779			
1	Inner Mongolia	5,080	9	Hunan	551
2	Yunnan	2,107	10	Jiangxi	526
3	Guangdong	1,286	11	Tibet	469
4	Sichuan	907	12	Fujian	341
5	Xinjiang	810	13	Shaanxi	307
6	Gansu	776	14	Guangxi	260
7	Henan	578	15	Jiangsu	259
8	Qinghai	560	16	Hebei	228

Ensured Reserves of Zinc

Metal, Thousand Tons

National Total		37,662			
1	Inner Mongolia	9,623	9	Fujian	804
2	Yunnan	9,053	10	Hebei	764
3	Gansu	3,137	11	Jiangxi	764
4	Sichuan	2,318	12	Hunan	759
5	Guangdong	2,286	13	Shaanxi	732
6	Xinjiang	1,680	14	Guizhou	712
7	Qinghai	1,155	15	Henan	475
8	Guangxi	1,061	16	Liaoning	448

Ensured Reserves of Bauxite

Ore, Thousand Tons

National Total	983,235			
1 Guangxi	466,318	7	Hubei	5,029
2 Shanxi	151,228	8	Hunan	3,114
3 Henan	143,768	9	Shandong	1,589
4 Guizhou	132,050	10	Sichuan	516
5 Chongqing	64,483	11	Hebei	280
6 Yunnan	14,852	12	Shaanxi	9

Ensured Reserves of Pyrite Ore

Ore, Thousand Tons, 2014

National Total	1,301,941			
1 Sichuan	377,270	9	Hubei	47,221
2 Guangdong	162,146	10	Chongqing	14,531
3 Inner Mongolia	160,393	11	Liaoning	12,721
4 Jiangxi	148,860	12	Hebei	11,428
5 Anhui	143,813	13	Fujian	11,070
6 Henan	59,919	14	Shanxi	10,581
7 Guizhou	55,945	15	Guangxi	8,371
8 Yunnan	48,789	16	Hunan	7,885

Ensured Reserves of Phosphorus Ore

Ore, Million Tons

National Total	3,024			
1 Hubei	770	9	Qinghai	60
2 Yunnan	649	10	Hunan	24
3 Guizhou	605	11	Anhui	20
4 Sichuan	455	12	Jiangsu	13
5 Hebei	194	13	Shaanxi	6

6	Liaoning	81	14	Inner Mongolia	2
7	Shanxi	81	15	Henan	2
8	Jiangxi	61	16	Ningxia	1

Ensured Reserves of Kaolin Ore

Ore, Thousand Tons

National Total		496,497			
1	Guangxi	236,056	9	Liaoning	5,369
2	Guangdong	54,086	10	Hubei	4,604
3	Fujian	53,663	11	Yunnan	4,023
4	Inner Mongolia	48,147	12	Shandong	3,360
5	Jiangxi	31,770	13	Jiangsu	1,677
6	Hunan	20,154	14	Anhui	1,660
7	Hainan	19,176	15	Shanxi	1,602
8	Zhejiang	8,403	16	Shaanxi	811

Ensured Reserves of Magnesite Ore

Ore, Thousand Tons

National Total		1,207,475
1	Liaoning	1,048,342
2	Shandong	147,935
3	Hebei	8,823
4	Sichuan	1,865
5	Qinghai	499
6	Jilin	11

Per Capita Water Resources

cu. m/Person

1	Tibet	142,531	9	Jiangxi	3,155
2	Qinghai	11,217	10	Fujian	3,063

3	Hainan	5,637	11	Sichuan	3,053
4	Guangxi	4,377	12	Hunan	2,374
5	Xinjiang	4,252	13	Jilin	2,208
6	Inner Mongolia	3,849	14	Guizhou	2,174
7	Heilongjiang	3,702	15	Guangdong	2,131
8	Yunnan	3,652	16	Zhejiang	1,697

Waste Water Discharged

Thousand Tons

National Total   69,544,327

1	Guangdong	8,624,711	9	Hubei	2,940,540
2	Jiangsu	5,943,591	10	Anhui	2,662,342
3	Shandong	4,945,702	11	Fujian	2,590,979
4	Zhejiang	4,191,203	12	Liaoning	2,345,082
5	Henan	4,125,818	13	Guangxi	2,253,027
6	Hebei	3,109,205	14	Shanghai	2,229,629
7	Sichuan	3,076,478	15	Jiangxi	2,071,376
8	Hunan	3,072,270	16	Yunnan	1,565,833

Sulfur Dioxide Emission in Waste Gas

Tons

National Total   20,439

1	Shandong	1,645	9	Xinjiang	829
2	Inner Mongolia	1,359	10	Sichuan	817
3	Hebei	1,285	11	Shaanxi	806
4	Shanxi	1,255	12	Guangdong	762
5	Henan	1,254	13	Yunnan	663
6	Liaoning	1,027	14	Hunan	641
7	Guizhou	986	15	Hubei	599
8	Jiangsu	942	16	Zhejiang	593

Nitrogen Oxides Emission in Waste Gas

Tons

	National Total	22,274			
1	Hebei	1,652	9	Xinjiang	887
2	Shandong	1,651	10	Anhui	864
3	Henan	1,566	11	Shaanxi	759
4	Inner Mongolia	1,378	12	Zhejiang	753
5	Jiangsu	1,338	13	Heilongjiang	752
6	Guangdong	1,204	14	Sichuan	624
7	Shanxi	1,158	15	Hubei	612
8	Liaoning	955	16	Hunan	588

Smoke and Dust Emission in Waste Gas

Tons

	National Total	12,781			
1	Hebei	1,313	9	Shaanxi	538
2	Shanxi	1,027	10	Jiangsu	500
3	Inner Mongolia	822	11	Anhui	419
4	Xinjiang	756	12	Yunnan	387
5	Heilongjiang	722	13	Hubei	360
6	Shandong	697	14	Hunan	359
7	Liaoning	671	15	Jiangxi	356
8	Henan	641	16	Guangdong	354

Wastes Collected and Transported

Thousand Tons

	National Total	172,386			
1	Guangdong	20,921	9	Shanghai	7,350
2	Jiangsu	12,027	10	Beijing	6,717
3	Zhejiang	11,233	11	Hunan	6,168

4	Shandong	10,074	12	Hebei	5,853
5	Liaoning	9,271	13	Heilongjiang	5,819
6	Henan	8,056	14	Fujian	5,518
7	Sichuan	7,507	15	Jilin	4,854
8	Hubei	7,458	16	Anhui	4,559

Highest Forest Coverage Rate

%

National Total		21.63			
1	Fujian	65.95	9	Heilongjiang	43.16
2	Jiangxi	60.01	10	Shaanxi	41.42
3	Zhejiang	59.07	11	Jilin	40.38
4	Guangxi	56.51	12	Chongqing	38.43
5	Hainan	55.38	13	Hubei	38.40
6	Guangdong	51.26	14	Liaoning	38.24
7	Yunnan	50.03	15	Guizhou	37.09
8	Hunan	47.77	16	Beijing	35.84

Area of Grassland

Thousand Hectares

National Total		392,833			
1	Tibet	82,052	9	Heilongjiang	7,532
2	Inner Mongolia	78,804	10	Hunan	6,373
3	Xinjiang	57,259	11	Hubei	6,352
4	Qinghai	36,370	12	Jilin	5,842
5	Sichuan	20,380	13	Shaanxi	5,206
6	Gansu	17,904	14	Hebei	4,712
7	Yunnan	15,308	15	Shanxi	4,552
8	Guangxi	8,698	16	Jiangxi	4,442

Area of Wetlands

Thousand Hectares

	National Total	53,603			
1	Qinghai	8,144	9	Shandong	1,738
2	Tibet	6,529	10	Gansu	1,694
3	Inner Mongolia	6,011	11	Hubei	1,445
4	Heilongjiang	5,143	12	Liaoning	1,395
5	Xinjiang	3,948	13	Zhejiang	1,110
6	Jiangsu	2,823	14	Anhui	1,042
7	Guangdong	1,753	15	Hunan	1,020
8	Sichuan	1,748	16	Jilin	998

Highest Proportion of Wetlands of Territory

%

	National Total	5.56			
1	Shanghai	73.27	9	Liaoning	9.42
2	Jiangsu	27.51	10	Hainan	9.14
3	Tianjin	23.94	11	Hubei	7.77
4	Heilongjiang	11.31	12	Anhui	7.46
5	Qinghai	11.27	13	Fujian	7.18
6	Shandong	11.07	14	Jiangxi	5.45
7	Zhejiang	10.91	15	Tibet	5.35
8	Guangdong	9.76	16	Jilin	5.32

Area of Nature Reserves

Thousand Hectares

	National Total	146,310			
1	Tibet	41,369	9	Liaoning	2,805
2	Qinghai	21,765	10	Hainan	2,735
3	Xinjiang	19,483	11	Jilin	2,430

4	Inner Mongolia	13,689	12	Guangdong	1,850
5	Sichuan	8,978	13	Guangxi	1,456
6	Gansu	7,463	14	Hunan	1,284
7	Heilongjiang	6,806	15	Jiangxi	1,246
8	Yunnan	2,857	16	Shaanxi	1,166

Culture and Recreation

Highest Electricity Consumption

Million Kwh

1	Jiangsu	495,662	9	Sichuan	194,895
2	Guangdong	483,013	10	Shanxi	183,235
3	Shandong	408,312	11	Fujian	170,073
4	Zhejiang	345,305	12	Hubei	162,975
5	Hebei	325,119	13	Xinjiang	153,975
6	Henan	289,918	14	Anhui	152,807
7	Inner Mongolia	218,190	15	Yunnan	145,981
8	Liaoning	200,846	16	Hunan	142,309

Population Coverage Rate of Radio Programs

%

National Total	97.79			
1	Beijing	100.00	9	Liaoning	98.63
2	Tianjin	100.00	10	Heilongjiang	98.60
3	Shanghai	100.00	11	Jilin	98.59
4	Jiangsu	99.99	12	Shandong	98.49
5	Guangdong	99.90	13	Anhui	98.34
6	Zhejiang	99.56	14	Chongqing	98.30
7	Hebei	99.34	15	Inner Mongolia	98.25
8	Hubei	98.80	16	Fujian	98.20

Population Coverage Rate of TV Programs

%

National Total	98.42			
1	Beijing	100.00	9	Chongqing	98.88
2	Tianjin	100.00	10	Hubei	98.81

3	Shanghai	100.00	11	Heilongjiang	98.80
4	Guangdong	99.90	12	Liaoning	98.72
5	Jiangsu	99.88	13	Jilin	98.71
6	Zhejiang	99.64	14	Fujian	98.63
7	Hebei	99.27	15	Anhui	98.57
8	Ningxia	99.09	16	Jiangxi	98.50

Art Performance Places Attendances

10,000 Person-times

National Total		7,776			
1	Jiangsu	2,160	9	Shaanxi	248
2	Zhejiang	894	10	Henan	229
3	Shanxi	517	11	Fujian	223
4	Hunan	329	12	Shanghai	215
5	Guangdong	315	13	Beijing	210
6	Shandong	299	14	Hebei	204
7	Anhui	259	15	Jiangxi	204
8	Hubei	256	16	Jilin	179

Collections of Public Libraries Owned Per Person

Copy

National Total		0.55			
1	Shanghai	3.00	9	Fujian	0.65
2	Tianjin	1.00	10	Jilin	0.58
3	Beijing	0.98	11	Guangdong	0.57
4	Zhejiang	0.94	12	Xinjiang	0.55
5	Ningxia	0.91	13	Inner Mongolia	0.53
6	Liaoning	0.76	14	Heilongjiang	0.48
7	Jiangsu	0.73	15	Gansu	0.47
8	Qinghai	0.66	16	Hubei	0.46

Museums Attendances

Thousand Person-times

National Total	637,760			
1	Jiangsu	61,180		
2	Sichuan	48,340		
3	Shandong	43,360		
4	Henan	41,810		
5	Zhejiang	37,890		
6	Guangdong	35,990		
7	Shaanxi	28,750		
8	Hunan	28,360		

9	Jiangxi	26,570
10	Hebei	24,800
11	Hubei	23,580
12	Fujian	21,250
13	Anhui	20,370
14	Chongqing	19,160
15	Heilongjiang	18,240
16	Shanghai	17,680

Traffic Accidents

Number of Traffic Accidents

Case

	National Total	198,394			
1	Guangdong	25,424	9	Henan	6,449
2	Zhejiang	18,298	10	Shaanxi	5,952
3	Anhui	17,610	11	Hubei	5,798
4	Jiangsu	13,395	12	Liaoning	5,777
5	Shandong	12,879	13	Chongqing	5,642
6	Sichuan	9,571	14	Shanxi	5,303
7	Hunan	8,699	15	Hebei	5,204
8	Fujian	8,521	16	Xinjiang	4,944

Number of Deaths in Traffic Accidents

Person

	National Total	58,539			
1	Guangdong	5,647	9	Fujian	2,138
2	Zhejiang	4,860	10	Shanxi	2,133
3	Jiangsu	4,679	11	Liaoning	2,015
4	Shandong	3,748	12	Xinjiang	1,929
5	Anhui	2,669	13	Hunan	1,882
6	Sichuan	2,658	14	Hubei	1,801
7	Hebei	2,501	15	Shaanxi	1,800
8	Guangxi	2,172	16	Yunnan	1,747

Injuries in Traffic Accidents

Number

	National Total	213,724			
1	Guangdong	28,435	9	Chongqing	7,883
2	Anhui	20,343	10	Henan	6,569
3	Zhejiang	18,558	11	Hubei	6,353
4	Jiangsu	12,177	12	Xinjiang	5,647
5	Shandong	11,971	13	Liaoning	5,527
6	Sichuan	11,414	14	Shanxi	5,520
7	Hunan	11,293	15	Shaanxi	5,452
8	Fujian	9,501	16	Tianjin	4,920

People's Living

Household Consumption Expenditure

Yuan

1	Shanghai	39,223	9	Fujian	17,115
2	Beijing	33,337	10	Shandong	16,728
3	Tianjin	26,261	11	Chongqing	15,270
4	Zhejiang	24,771	12	Hubei	13,912
5	Guangdong	23,739	13	Jilin	13,676
6	Jiangsu	23,585	14	Ningxia	13,537
7	Liaoning	20,156	15	Shaanxi	13,206
8	Inner Mongolia	17,168	16	Heilongjiang	12,978

Part 3

Province Profiles

Provinces

Beijing

Capital City	Beijing		
Total Rainfall (mm)*	579	Av. Temperature (°C)	12.8
Total Sunshine Hours	2,371	Av. Humidity (%)	55

Economic Indicators

		Origins of GDP (%)	
GDP (¥ billion)	1,950		
GDP ($ billion)	314.9	Agriculture	0.8
GDP per head (¥)	93,213	Industry	22.3
External Trade of Goods ($ billion)	131,561	Services	76.9

Social Indicators

Population ('000)	21,148	Urban population (%)	86.3
Per Capita Income (¥)	40,830	Pop. Growth Rate (‰)	4.4
No. of Households	6,166	Av. No. per Household	2.61
Children Dependency Ratio	12.2	Old Dependency Ratio	10.5
Public Health Spending (% of GDP)	1.4	Public Education Spending (% of GDP)	3.5
Doctors per 1,000 pop.	5.9	Cars per 1,000 pop.	201
TV households, % with cable	125	Mobile Telephone Subscribers per 100 pop.	159.5
Telephone lines per 100 pop.	41.0	Broadband Subscribers of Internet per 100 pop.	22.7

---

* Figures of rainfall, sunshine hours, temperature, and humidity in this part refer to the statistical data of the capital city.

Tianjin

Capital City	Tianjin		
Total Rainfall (mm)	412	Av. Temperature (°C)	12.8
Total Sunshine Hours	2,255	Av. Humidity (%)	59
Economic Indicators			
GDP (¥ billion)	1,437	Origins of GDP (%)	
GDP ($ billion)	232.0	Agriculture	1.3
GDP per head (¥)	99,607	Industry	50.6
External Trade of Goods ($ billion)	134,600	Services	48.1
Social Indicators			
Population ('000)	14,722	Urban population (%)	82.0
Per Capita Income (¥)	26,359	Pop. Growth Rate (‰)	2.3
No. of Households	4,515	Av. No. per Household	2.67
Children Dependency Ratio	14.5	Old Dependency Ratio	14.8
Public Health Spending (% of GDP)	0.9	Public Education Spending (% of GDP)	3.2
Doctors per 1,000 pop.	3.2	Cars per 1,000 pop.	152
TV households, % with cable	83	Mobile Telephone Subscribers per 100 pop.	90
Telephone lines per 100 pop.	41.0	Broadband Subscribers of Internet per 100 pop.	12.8

Hebei

Capital City	Shijiazhuang		
Total Rainfall (mm)	508	Av. Temperature (°C)	13.8
Total Sunshine Hours	1,717	Av. Humidity (%)	60

Economic Indicators

GDP (¥ billion)	2,830	Origins of GDP (%)	
GDP ($ billion)	457.0	Agriculture	12.4
GDP per head (¥)	38,716	Industry	52.2
External Trade of Goods ($ billion)	90,219	Services	35.5

Social Indicators

Population ('000)	73,326	Urban population (%)	48.1
Per Capita Income (¥)	15,190	Pop. Growth Rate (‰)	6.2
No. of Households	19,036	Av. No. per Household	3.17
Children Dependency Ratio	24.4	Old Dependency Ratio	12.6
Public Health Spending (% of GDP)	1.3	Public Education Spending (% of GDP)	3.0
Doctors per 1,000 pop.	2.0	Cars per 1,000 pop.	98
TV households, % with cable	38	Mobile Telephone Subscribers per 100 pop.	82
Telephone lines per 100 pop.	15.7	Broadband Subscribers of Internet per 100 pop.	14.1

Shanxi

Capital City	Taiyuan		
Total Rainfall (mm)	487	Av. Temperature (°C)	11.2
Total Sunshine Hours	2,627	Av. Humidity (%)	56
Economic Indicators			
GDP (¥ billion)	1,260	Origins of GDP (%)	
GDP ($ billion)	203.5	Agriculture	6.1
GDP per head (¥)	34,813	Industry	53.9
External Trade of Goods ($ billion)	17,161	Services	40.0
Social Indicators			
Population ('000)	36,298	Urban population (%)	52.6
Per Capita Income (¥)	15,120	Pop. Growth Rate (‰)	5.2
No. of Households	9,903	Av. No. per Household	3.01
Children Dependency Ratio	20.6	Old Dependency Ratio	10.5
Public Health Spending (% of GDP)	1.6	Public Education Spending (% of GDP)	4.3
Doctors per 1,000 pop.	2.5	Cars per 1,000 pop.	88
TV households, % with cable	39	Mobile Telephone Subscribers per 100 pop.	86
Telephone lines per 100 pop.	16.1	Broadband Subscribers of Internet per 100 pop.	14.4

Inner Mongolia

Capital City	Hohhot		
Total Rainfall (mm)	565	Av. Temperature (°C)	7.3
Total Sunshine Hours	2,630	Av. Humidity (%)	50
Economic Indicators			
GDP (¥ billion)	1,683	Origins of GDP (%)	
GDP ($ billion)	271.8	Agriculture	9.5
GDP per head (¥)	67,498	Industry	54.0
External Trade of Goods ($ billion)	14,389	Services	36.5
Social Indicators			
Population ('000)	24,976	Urban population (%)	58.7
Per Capita Income (¥)	18,693	Pop. Growth Rate (‰)	3.4
No. of Households	7,521	Av. No. per Household	2.74
Children Dependency Ratio	17.7	Old Dependency Ratio	11.0
Public Health Spending (% of GDP)	1.2	Public Education Spending (% of GDP)	2.7
Doctors per 1,000 pop.	2.5	Cars per 1,000 pop.	106
TV households, % with cable	38	Mobile Telephone Subscribers per 100 pop.	108
Telephone lines per 100 pop.	15.1	Broadband Subscribers of Internet per 100 pop.	11.4

Liaoning

Capital City	Shenyang		
Total Rainfall (mm)	788	Av. Temperature (°C)	7.9
Total Sunshine Hours	2,390	Av. Humidity (%)	68

Economic Indicators

GDP (¥ billion)	2,708	Origins of GDP (%)	
GDP ($ billion)	437.2	Agriculture	8.6
GDP per head (¥)	61,686	Industry	52.7
External Trade of Goods ($ billion)	121,361	Services	38.7

Social Indicators

Population ('000)	43,900	Urban population (%)	66.5
Per Capita Income (¥)	20,818	Pop. Growth Rate (‰)	0.0
No. of Households	13,106	Av. No. per Household	2.72
Children Dependency Ratio	13.1	Old Dependency Ratio	12.9
Public Health Spending (% of GDP)	0.8	Public Education Spending (% of GDP)	2.5
Doctors per 1,000 pop.	2.4	Cars per 1,000 pop.	81
TV households, % with cable	66	Mobile Telephone Subscribers per 100 pop.	104
Telephone lines per 100 pop.	27.8	Broadband Subscribers of Internet per 100 pop.	16.6

Jilin

Capital City	Changchun		
Total Rainfall (mm)	737	Av. Temperature (°C)	5.6
Total Sunshine Hours	2,396	Av. Humidity (%)	64

Economic Indicators

GDP (¥ billion)	1,298	Origins of GDP (%)	
GDP ($ billion)	209.6	Agriculture	11.6
GDP per head (¥)	47,191	Industry	52.8
External Trade of Goods ($ billion)	25,191	Services	35.5

Social Indicators

Population ('000)	27,513	Urban population (%)	54.2
Per Capita Income (¥)	15,998	Pop. Growth Rate (‰)	0.3
No. of Households	8,206	Av. No. per Household	2.77
Children Dependency Ratio	15.0	Old Dependency Ratio	12.3
Public Health Spending (% of GDP)	1.4	Public Education Spending (% of GDP)	3.3
Doctors per 1,000 pop.	2.3	Cars per 1,000 pop.	75
TV households, % with cable	57	Mobile Telephone Subscribers per 100 pop.	86
Telephone lines per 100 pop.	21.0	Broadband Subscribers of Internet per 100 pop.	13.8

Heilongjiang

Capital City	Harbin		
Total Rainfall (mm)	634	Av. Temperature (°C)	4.3
Total Sunshine Hours	2,024	Av. Humidity (%)	68
Economic Indicators			
GDP (¥ billion)	1,438	Origins of GDP (%)	
GDP ($ billion)	232.2	Agriculture	17.5
GDP per head (¥)	37,509	Industry	41.1
External Trade of Goods ($ billion)	27,396	Services	41.4
Social Indicators			
Population ('000)	38,350	Urban population (%)	57.4
Per Capita Income (¥)	15,903	Pop. Growth Rate (‰)	0.8
No. of Households	11,554	Av. No. per Household	2.74
Children Dependency Ratio	15.2	Old Dependency Ratio	11.3
Public Health Spending (% of GDP)	1.3	Public Education Spending (% of GDP)	3.5
Doctors per 1,000 pop.	2.1	Cars per 1,000 pop.	60
TV households, % with cable	55	Mobile Telephone Subscribers per 100 pop.	79
Telephone lines per 100 pop.	19.5	Broadband Subscribers of Internet per 100 pop.	12.0

Shanghai

Capital City	Shanghai		
Total Rainfall (mm)	1,173	Av. Temperature (°C)	17.6
Total Sunshine Hours	1,865	Av. Humidity (%)	68
Economic Indicators			
GDP (¥ billion)	2,160	Origins of GDP (%)	
GDP ($ billion)	348.8	Agriculture	0.6
GDP per head (¥)	90,092	Industry	37.2
External Trade of Goods ($ billion)	434,278	Services	62.2
Social Indicators			
Population ('000)	24,152	Urban population (%)	89.6
Per Capita Income (¥)	42,174	Pop. Growth Rate (‰)	2.9
No. of Households	8,377	Av. No. per Household	2.35
Children Dependency Ratio	11.7	Old Dependency Ratio	13.3
Public Health Spending (% of GDP)	1.0	Public Education Spending (% of GDP)	3.1
Doctors per 1,000 pop.	4.0	Cars per 1,000 pop.	68
TV households, % with cable	130	Mobile Telephone Subscribers per 100 pop.	133
Telephone lines per 100 pop.	36.0	Broadband Subscribers of Internet per 100 pop.	21.2

Jiangsu

Capital City	Nanjing		
Total Rainfall (mm)	898	Av. Temperature (°C)	16.8
Total Sunshine Hours	2,197	Av. Humidity (%)	68
Economic Indicators			
GDP (¥ billion)	5,916	Origins of GDP (%)	
GDP ($ billion)	955.3	Agriculture	6.2
GDP per head (¥)	74,607	Industry	49.2
External Trade of Goods ($ billion)	593,295	Services	44.7
Social Indicators			
Population ('000)	79,395	Urban population (%)	64.1
Per Capita Income (¥)	24,776	Pop. Growth Rate (‰)	2.4
No. of Households	22,008	Av. No. per Household	2.95
Children Dependency Ratio	17.9	Old Dependency Ratio	16.5
Public Health Spending (% of GDP)	0.8	Public Education Spending (% of GDP)	2.4
Doctors per 1,000 pop.	2.2	Cars per 1,000 pop.	98
TV households, % with cable	93	Mobile Telephone Subscribers per 100 pop.	100
Telephone lines per 100 pop.	28.8	Broadband Subscribers of Internet per 100 pop.	18.0

Zhejiang

Capital City	Hangzhou		
Total Rainfall (mm)	1,521	Av. Temperature (°C)	18.0
Total Sunshine Hours	1,666	Av. Humidity (%)	68
Economic Indicators			
GDP (¥ billion)	3,757	Origins of GDP (%)	
GDP ($ billion)	606.6	Agriculture	4.8
GDP per head (¥)	68,462	Industry	49.1
External Trade of Goods ($ billion)	365,508	Services	46.1
Social Indicators			
Population ('000)	54,980	Urban population (%)	64.0
Per Capita Income (¥)	29,775	Pop. Growth Rate (‰)	4.6
No. of Households	17,034	Av. No. per Household	2.54
Children Dependency Ratio	15.1	Old Dependency Ratio	11.7
Public Health Spending (% of GDP)	0.9	Public Education Spending (% of GDP)	2.5
Doctors per 1,000 pop.	2.9	Cars per 1,000 pop.	139
TV households, % with cable	90	Mobile Telephone Subscribers per 100 pop.	129
Telephone lines per 100 pop.	32.4	Broadband Subscribers of Internet per 100 pop.	22.6

Anhui

Capital City	Hefei		
Total Rainfall (mm)	893	Av. Temperature (°C)	17.0
Total Sunshine Hours	1,971	Av. Humidity (%)	76
Economic Indicators			
GDP (¥ billion)	1,904	Origins of GDP (%)	
GDP ($ billion)	307.4	Agriculture	12.3
GDP per head (¥)	31,684	Industry	54.6
External Trade of Goods ($ billion)	38,928	Services	33.0
Social Indicators			
Population ('000)	60,298	Urban population (%)	47.9
Per Capita Income (¥)	15,154	Pop. Growth Rate (‰)	6.8
No. of Households	16,155	Av. No. per Household	3.03
Children Dependency Ratio	26.0	Old Dependency Ratio	14.8
Public Health Spending (% of GDP)	1.9	Public Education Spending (% of GDP)	3.9
Doctors per 1,000 pop.	1.4	Cars per 1,000 pop.	46
TV households, % with cable	33	Mobile Telephone Subscribers per 100 pop.	66
Telephone lines per 100 pop.	16.2	Broadband Subscribers of Internet per 100 pop.	9.1

Fujian

Capital City	Fuzhou		
Total Rainfall (mm)	1,138	Av. Temperature (°C)	20.4
Total Sunshine Hours	1,578	Av. Humidity (%)	72
Economic Indicators			
GDP (¥ billion)	2,176	Origins of GDP (%)	
GDP ($ billion)	351.3	Agriculture	8.9
GDP per head (¥)	57,856	Industry	52.0
External Trade of Goods ($ billion)	154,483	Services	39.1
Social Indicators			
Population ('000)	37,740	Urban population (%)	60.8
Per Capita Income (¥)	21,218	Pop. Growth Rate (‰)	6.2
No. of Households	11,340	Av. No. per Household	2.72
Children Dependency Ratio	22.5	Old Dependency Ratio	10.9
Public Health Spending (% of GDP)	1.0	Public Education Spending (% of GDP)	2.6
Doctors per 1,000 pop.	2.0	Cars per 1,000 pop.	74
TV households, % with cable	67	Mobile Telephone Subscribers per 100 pop.	114
Telephone lines per 100 pop.	26.1	Broadband Subscribers of Internet per 100 pop.	22.1

Jiangxi

Capital City	Nanchang		
Total Rainfall (mm)	1,432	Av. Temperature (°C)	19.0
Total Sunshine Hours	2,034	Av. Humidity (%)	73
Economic Indicators			
GDP (¥ billion)	1,434	Origins of GDP (%)	
GDP ($ billion)	231.5	Agriculture	11.4
GDP per head (¥)	31,771	Industry	53.5
External Trade of Goods ($ billion)	33,652	Services	35.1
Social Indicators			
Population ('000)	45,222	Urban population (%)	48.9
Per Capita Income (¥)	15,100	Pop. Growth Rate (‰)	6.9
No. of Households	10,730	Av. No. per Household	3.42
Children Dependency Ratio	27.6	Old Dependency Ratio	12.6
Public Health Spending (% of GDP)	1.8	Public Education Spending (% of GDP)	4.6
Doctors per 1,000 pop.	1.5	Cars per 1,000 pop.	42
TV households, % with cable	48	Mobile Telephone Subscribers per 100 pop.	62
Telephone lines per 100 pop.	13.8	Broadband Subscribers of Internet per 100 pop.	9.1

Shandong

Capital City	Jinan		
Total Rainfall (mm)	736	Av. Temperature (°C)	14.7
Total Sunshine Hours	2,408	Av. Humidity (%)	57
Economic Indicators			
GDP (¥ billion)	5,468	Origins of GDP (%)	
GDP ($ billion)	883.0	Agriculture	8.7
GDP per head (¥)	56,323	Industry	50.1
External Trade of Goods ($ billion)	314,942	Services	41.2
Social Indicators			
Population ('000)	97,334	Urban population (%)	53.8
Per Capita Income (¥)	19,008	Pop. Growth Rate (‰)	5.0
No. of Households	28,638	Av. No. per Household	2.80
Children Dependency Ratio	21.0	Old Dependency Ratio	14.9
Public Health Spending (% of GDP)	0.9	Public Education Spending (% of GDP)	2.6
Doctors per 1,000 pop.	2.4	Cars per 1,000 pop.	107
TV households, % with cable	62	Mobile Telephone Subscribers per 100 pop.	86
Telephone lines per 100 pop.	17.5	Broadband Subscribers of Internet per 100 pop.	15.1

Henan

Capital City	Zhengzhou		
Total Rainfall (mm)	353	Av. Temperature (°C)	16.1
Total Sunshine Hours	1,926	Av. Humidity (%)	53

Economic Indicators

GDP (¥ billion)	3,216	Origins of GDP (%)	
GDP ($ billion)	519.2	Agriculture	12.6
GDP per head (¥)	34,174	Industry	55.4
External Trade of Goods ($ billion)	62,774	Services	32.0

Social Indicators

Population ('000)	94,134	Urban population (%)	43.8
Per Capita Income (¥)	14,204	Pop. Growth Rate (‰)	5.5
No. of Households	23,644	Av. No. per Household	3.28
Children Dependency Ratio	29.5	Old Dependency Ratio	12.7
Public Health Spending (% of GDP)	1.5	Public Education Spending (% of GDP)	3.6
Doctors per 1,000 pop.	1.6	Cars per 1,000 pop.	62
TV households, % with cable	33	Mobile Telephone Subscribers per 100 pop.	76
Telephone lines per 100 pop.	13.0	Broadband Subscribers of Internet per 100 pop.	10.6

Hubei

Capital City	Wuhan		
Total Rainfall (mm)	1,434	Av. Temperature (°C)	17.1
Total Sunshine Hours	2,093	Av. Humidity (%)	77

Economic Indicators

		Origins of GDP (%)	
GDP (¥ billion)	2,467		
GDP ($ billion)	398.3	Agriculture	12.6
GDP per head (¥)	42,613	Industry	49.3
External Trade of Goods ($ billion)	35,635	Services	38.1

Social Indicators

Population ('000)	57,990	Urban population (%)	54.5
Per Capita Income (¥)	16,472	Pop. Growth Rate (‰)	4.9
No. of Households	15,907	Av. No. per Household	2.94
Children Dependency Ratio	19.9	Old Dependency Ratio	13.2
Public Health Spending (% of GDP)	1.3	Public Education Spending (% of GDP)	2.8
Doctors per 1,000 pop.	1.9	Cars per 1,000 pop.	49
TV households, % with cable	51	Mobile Telephone Subscribers per 100 pop.	76
Telephone lines per 100 pop.	17.0	Broadband Subscribers of Internet per 100 pop.	14.0

Hunan

Capital City	Changsha		
Total Rainfall (mm)	1,255	Av. Temperature (°C)	19.2
Total Sunshine Hours	2,050	Av. Humidity (%)	67
Economic Indicators			
GDP (¥ billion)	2,450	Origins of GDP (%)	
GDP ($ billion)	395.6	Agriculture	12.6
GDP per head (¥)	36,763	Industry	47.0
External Trade of Goods ($ billion)	24,316	Services	40.3
Social Indicators			
Population ('000)	66,906	Urban population (%)	48.0
Per Capita Income (¥)	16,005	Pop. Growth Rate (‰)	6.5
No. of Households	16,935	Av. No. per Household	3.25
Children Dependency Ratio	25.7	Old Dependency Ratio	14.9
Public Health Spending (% of GDP)	1.4	Public Education Spending (% of GDP)	3.3
Doctors per 1,000 pop.	1.8	Cars per 1,000 pop.	48
TV households, % with cable	42	Mobile Telephone Subscribers per 100 pop.	68
Telephone lines per 100 pop.	13.7	Broadband Subscribers of Internet per 100 pop.	10.5

Guangdong

Capital City	Guangzhou		
Total Rainfall (mm)	2,095	Av. Temperature (°C)	21.5
Total Sunshine Hours	1,583	Av. Humidity (%)	81

Economic Indicators

		Origins of GDP (%)	
GDP (¥ billion)	6,216	Origins of GDP (%)	
GDP ($ billion)	1,003.7	Agriculture	4.9
GDP per head (¥)	58,540	Industry	47.3
External Trade of Goods ($ billion)	1,281,192	Services	47.8

Social Indicators

Population ('000)	106,440	Urban population (%)	67.8
Per Capita Income (¥)	23,421	Pop. Growth Rate (‰)	6.0
No. of Households	27,050	Av. No. per Household	3.15
Children Dependency Ratio	21.9	Old Dependency Ratio	9.5
Public Health Spending (% of GDP)	0.9	Public Education Spending (% of GDP)	2.8
Doctors per 1,000 pop.	2.4	Cars per 1,000 pop.	94
TV households, % with cable	81	Mobile Telephone Subscribers per 100 pop.	138
Telephone lines per 100 pop.	29.1	Broadband Subscribers of Internet per 100 pop.	19.6

Guangxi

Capital City	Nanning		
Total Rainfall (mm)	1,569	Av. Temperature (°C)	21.6
Total Sunshine Hours	1,620	Av. Humidity (%)	80
Economic Indicators			
GDP (¥ billion)	1,438	Origins of GDP (%)	
GDP ($ billion)	232.2	Agriculture	16.3
GDP per head (¥)	30,588	Industry	47.7
External Trade of Goods ($ billion)	38,696	Services	36.0
Social Indicators			
Population ('000)	47,190	Urban population (%)	44.8
Per Capita Income (¥)	14,082	Pop. Growth Rate (‰)	7.9
No. of Households	11,809	Av. No. per Household	3.31
Children Dependency Ratio	31.0	Old Dependency Ratio	13.4
Public Health Spending (% of GDP)	2.0	Public Education Spending (% of GDP)	4.2
Doctors per 1,000 pop.	1.5	Cars per 1,000 pop.	47
TV households, % with cable	46	Mobile Telephone Subscribers per 100 pop.	62
Telephone lines per 100 pop.	10.3	Broadband Subscribers of Internet per 100 pop.	11.9

Hainan

Capital City	Haikou		
Total Rainfall (mm)	2,067	Av. Temperature (°C)	24.3
Total Sunshine Hours	1,726	Av. Humidity (%)	82

Economic Indicators

GDP (¥ billion)	315	Origins of GDP (%)	
GDP ($ billion)	50.8	Agriculture	24.0
GDP per head (¥)	35,317	Industry	27.7
External Trade of Goods ($ billion)	14,758	Services	48.3

Social Indicators

Population ('000)	8,953	Urban population (%)	52.7
Per Capita Income (¥)	15,733	Pop. Growth Rate (‰)	8.7
No. of Households	2,060	Av. No. per Household	3.52
Children Dependency Ratio	25.6	Old Dependency Ratio	11.2
Public Health Spending (% of GDP)	2.2	Public Education Spending (% of GDP)	5.5
Doctors per 1,000 pop.	1.8	Cars per 1,000 pop.	57
TV households, % with cable	43	Mobile Telephone Subscribers per 100 pop.	96
Telephone lines per 100 pop.	19.4	Broadband Subscribers of Internet per 100 pop.	12.4

Chongqing

Capital City	Chongqing		
Total Rainfall (mm)	1,027	Av. Temperature (°C)	19.8
Total Sunshine Hours	1,214	Av. Humidity (%)	71

Economic Indicators

		Origins of GDP (%)	
GDP (¥ billion)	1,266	Origins of GDP (%)	
GDP ($ billion)	204.4	Agriculture	8.0
GDP per head (¥)	42,795	Industry	50.5
External Trade of Goods ($ billion)	58,785	Services	41.4

Social Indicators

Population ('000)	29,700	Urban population (%)	58.3
Per Capita Income (¥)	16,569	Pop. Growth Rate (‰)	3.6
No. of Households	9,071	Av. No. per Household	2.66
Children Dependency Ratio	21.9	Old Dependency Ratio	18.6
Public Health Spending (% of GDP)	1.6	Public Education Spending (% of GDP)	3.5
Doctors per 1,000 pop.	1.6	Cars per 1,000 pop.	50
TV households, % with cable	43	Mobile Telephone Subscribers per 100 pop.	80
Telephone lines per 100 pop.	19.5	Broadband Subscribers of Internet per 100 pop.	14.8

Sichuan

Capital City	Chengdu		
Total Rainfall (mm)	1,343	Av. Temperature (°C)	16.9
Total Sunshine Hours	1,129	Av. Humidity (%)	77

Economic Indicators

GDP (¥ billion)	2,626	Origins of GDP (%)	
GDP ($ billion)	424.0	Agriculture	13.0
GDP per head (¥)	32,454	Industry	51.7
External Trade of Goods ($ billion)	55,095	Services	35.2

Social Indicators

Population ('000)	81,070	Urban population (%)	44.9
Per Capita Income (¥)	14,231	Pop. Growth Rate (‰)	3.0
No. of Households	24,136	Av. No. per Household	2.76
Children Dependency Ratio	23.4	Old Dependency Ratio	18.1
Public Health Spending (% of GDP)	1.9	Public Education Spending (% of GDP)	3.9
Doctors per 1,000 pop.	1.9	Cars per 1,000 pop.	60
TV households, % with cable	47	Mobile Telephone Subscribers per 100 pop.	78
Telephone lines per 100 pop.	16.2	Broadband Subscribers of Internet per 100 pop.	10.3

Guizhou

Capital City	Guiyang		
Total Rainfall (mm)	888	Av. Temperature (°C)	15.1
Total Sunshine Hours	1,231	Av. Humidity (%)	79

Economic Indicators

		Origins of GDP (%)	
GDP (¥ billion)	801		
GDP ($ billion)	129.3	Agriculture	12.9
GDP per head (¥)	22,922	Industry	40.5
External Trade of Goods ($ billion)	4,757	Services	46.6

Social Indicators

Population ('000)	35,022	Urban population (%)	37.8
Per Capita Income (¥)	11,083	Pop. Growth Rate (‰)	5.9
No. of Households	9,296	Av. No. per Household	3.07
Children Dependency Ratio	32.2	Old Dependency Ratio	13.5
Public Health Spending (% of GDP)	2.9	Public Education Spending (% of GDP)	7.0
Doctors per 1,000 pop.	1.3	Cars per 1,000 pop.	47
TV households, % with cable	32	Mobile Telephone Subscribers per 100 pop.	76
Telephone lines per 100 pop.	10.4	Broadband Subscribers of Internet per 100 pop.	8.3

Yunnan

Capital City	Kunming		
Total Rainfall (mm)	805	Av. Temperature (°C)	16.0
Total Sunshine Hours	2,513	Av. Humidity (%)	68
Economic Indicators			
GDP (¥ billion)	1,172	Origins of GDP (%)	
GDP ($ billion)	189.3	Agriculture	16.2
GDP per head (¥)	25,083	Industry	42.0
External Trade of Goods ($ billion)	15,824	Services	41.8
Social Indicators			
Population ('000)	46,866	Urban population (%)	40.5
Per Capita Income (¥)	12,578	Pop. Growth Rate (‰)	6.2
No. of Households	11,739	Av. No. per Household	3.28
Children Dependency Ratio	27.8	Old Dependency Ratio	11.1
Public Health Spending (% of GDP)	2.6	Public Education Spending (% of GDP)	5.9
Doctors per 1,000 pop.	1.6	Cars per 1,000 pop.	68
TV households, % with cable	37	Mobile Telephone Subscribers per 100 pop.	72
Telephone lines per 100 pop.	10.4	Broadband Subscribers of Internet per 100 pop.	8.6

Tibet

Capital City	Lhasa		
Total Rainfall (mm)	565	Av. Temperature (°C)	8.9
Total Sunshine Hours	3,047	Av. Humidity (%)	38
Economic Indicators			
GDP (¥ billion)	81	Origins of GDP (%)	
GDP ($ billion)	13.0	Agriculture	10.7
GDP per head (¥)	26,068	Industry	36.3
External Trade of Goods ($ billion)	2,104	Services	53.0
Social Indicators			
Population ('000)	3,120	Urban population (%)	23.7
Per Capita Income (¥)	9,747	Pop. Growth Rate (‰)	10.4
No. of Households	636	Av. No. per Household	4.05
Children Dependency Ratio	32.5	Old Dependency Ratio	7.2
Public Health Spending (% of GDP)	5.0	Public Education Spending (% of GDP)	13.3
Doctors per 1,000 pop.	1.6	Cars per 1,000 pop.	63
TV households, % with cable	30	Mobile Telephone Subscribers per 100 pop.	85
Telephone lines per 100 pop.	12.9	Broadband Subscribers of Internet per 100 pop.	6.1

Shaanxi

Capital City	Xi'an		
Total Rainfall (mm)	424	Av. Temperature (°C)	15.8
Total Sunshine Hours	2,191	Av. Humidity (%)	58
Economic Indicators			
GDP (¥ billion)	1,605	Origins of GDP (%)	
GDP ($ billion)	259.1	Agriculture	9.5
GDP per head (¥)	42,692	Industry	55.5
External Trade of Goods ($ billion)	20,220	Services	34.9
Social Indicators			
Population ('000)	37,640	Urban population (%)	51.3
Per Capita Income (¥)	14,372	Pop. Growth Rate (‰)	3.9
No. of Households	10,203	Av. No. per Household	3.05
Children Dependency Ratio	20.1	Old Dependency Ratio	13.1
Public Health Spending (% of GDP)	1.6	Public Education Spending (% of GDP)	4.4
Doctors per 1,000 pop.	1.9	Cars per 1,000 pop.	75
TV households, % with cable	51	Mobile Telephone Subscribers per 100 pop.	93
Telephone lines per 100 pop.	20.4	Broadband Subscribers of Internet per 100 pop.	13.4

Gansu

Capital City	Lanzhou		
Total Rainfall (mm)	256	Av. Temperature (°C)	8.3
Total Sunshine Hours	2,601	Av. Humidity (%)	53
Economic Indicators			
GDP (¥ billion)	627	Origins of GDP (%)	
GDP ($ billion)	101.2	Agriculture	14.0
GDP per head (¥)	24,296	Industry	45.0
External Trade of Goods ($ billion)	6,842	Services	41.0
Social Indicators			
Population ('000)	25,822	Urban population (%)	40.1
Per Capita Income (¥)	10,954	Pop. Growth Rate (‰)	6.1
No. of Households	6,280	Av. No. per Household	3.35
Children Dependency Ratio	22.8	Old Dependency Ratio	12.0
Public Health Spending (% of GDP)	2.6	Public Education Spending (% of GDP)	6.0
Doctors per 1,000 pop.	1.6	Cars per 1,000 pop.	44
TV households, % with cable	26	Mobile Telephone Subscribers per 100 pop.	77
Telephone lines per 100 pop.	14.1	Broadband Subscribers of Internet per 100 pop.	7.4

Qinghai

Capital City	Xining		
Total Rainfall (mm)	414	Av. Temperature (°C)	6.1
Total Sunshine Hours	2,661	Av. Humidity (%)	55
Economic Indicators			
GDP (¥ billion)	210	Origins of GDP (%)	
GDP ($ billion)	33.9	Agriculture	9.9
GDP per head (¥)	36,510	Industry	57.3
External Trade of Goods ($ billion)	856	Services	32.8
Social Indicators			
Population ('000)	5,778	Urban population (%)	48.5
Per Capita Income (¥)	12,948	Pop. Growth Rate (‰)	8.0
No. of Households	1,414	Av. No. per Household	3.37
Children Dependency Ratio	27.2	Old Dependency Ratio	9.8
Public Health Spending (% of GDP)	3.3	Public Education Spending (% of GDP)	5.8
Doctors per 1,000 pop.	2.3	Cars per 1,000 pop.	77
TV households, % with cable	38	Mobile Telephone Subscribers per 100 pop.	94
Telephone lines per 100 pop.	17.6	Broadband Subscribers of Internet per 100 pop.	9.5

Ningxia

Capital City	Yinchuan		
Total Rainfall (mm)	149	Av. Temperature (°C)	11.2
Total Sunshine Hours	2,694	Av. Humidity (%)	43
Economic Indicators			
GDP (¥ billion)	257	Origins of GDP (%)	
GDP ($ billion)	41.4	Agriculture	8.7
GDP per head (¥)	39,420	Industry	49.3
External Trade of Goods ($ billion)	2,608	Services	42.0
Social Indicators			
Population ('000)	6,542	Urban population (%)	52.0
Per Capita Income (¥)	14,566	Pop. Growth Rate (‰)	8.6
No. of Households	1,684	Av. No. per Household	3.20
Children Dependency Ratio	27.9	Old Dependency Ratio	9.7
Public Health Spending (% of GDP)	2.1	Public Education Spending (% of GDP)	4.4
Doctors per 1,000 pop.	2.1	Cars per 1,000 pop.	100
TV households, % with cable	46	Mobile Telephone Subscribers per 100 pop.	96
Telephone lines per 100 pop.	16.0	Broadband Subscribers of Internet per 100 pop.	10.9

Xinjiang

Capital City	Urumqi		
Total Rainfall (mm)	301	Av. Temperature (°C)	8.7
Total Sunshine Hours	3,069	Av. Humidity (%)	58
Economic Indicators			
GDP (¥ billion)	836	Origins of GDP (%)	
GDP ($ billion)	135.0	Agriculture	17.6
GDP per head (¥)	37,181	Industry	45.0
External Trade of Goods ($ billion)	37,568	Services	37.4
Social Indicators			
Population ('000)	22,643	Urban population (%)	44.5
Per Capita Income (¥)	13,670	Pop. Growth Rate (‰)	10.9
No. of Households	5,634	Av. No. per Household	3.30
Children Dependency Ratio	28.6	Old Dependency Ratio	8.8
Public Health Spending (% of GDP)	1.9	Public Education Spending (% of GDP)	6.4
Doctors per 1,000 pop.	2.3	Cars per 1,000 pop.	76
TV households, % with cable	33	Mobile Telephone Subscribers per 100 pop.	94
Telephone lines per 100 pop.	22.9	Broadband Subscribers of Internet per 100 pop.	12.9

Appendix

Hong Kong

Area (sq. km)	1,104	Currency	HKD
Total Rainfall (mm)	2,847	Av. Temperature (°C)	23.3
Total Sunshine Hours	1,770	Av. Humidity (%)	78

Economic Indicators

GDP (HKD billion)	2,125	Origins of GDP (%, 2012)	
GDP ($ billion)	274	Agriculture	0.05
GDP per head ($)	38,125	Industry	6.93
External Trade of Goods ($ billion)	983	Services	93.02

Social Indicators

Population ('000)	7,188	Pop. Growth Rate (‰)	2.0
Labour Force ('000)	3,859	Unemployment Rate (%)	3.4
No. of Households	2,404,800	Av. No. per Household	2.9
Children Dependency Ratio	14.9	Old Dependency Ratio	19.0
Public Health Spending (% of GDP)	1.7	Public Education Spending (% of GDP)	2.2
Doctors per 1,000 pop.	1.8	Beds per 1,000 pop.	5.1
Cars per 1,000 pop.	66	Life expectancy	

| Telephone lines per 100 pop. | 60 | Male | 80.9 |
| Broadband Subscribers of Internet per 100 pop. | 31 | Female | 86.6 |

Macao

Area (sq. km)	30.3	Currency	MOP
Total Rainfall (mm)	2,565	Av. Temperature (°C)	22.4
Total Sunshine Hours	1,724	Av. Humidity (%)	81

Economic Indicators

GDP (MOP billion)	413	Origins of GDP (%, 2012)	
GDP ($ billion)	51.8	Agriculture	0.00
GDP per head ($)	87,306	Industry	6.25
External Trade of Goods ($ billion)	11.3	Services	93.75

Social Indicators

Population ('000)	592	Pop. Growth Rate (‰)	7.9
Labour Force ('000)	368.0	Unemployment Rate (%)	1.8
Employed Persons ('000)	361.0	Children Dependency Ratio	14.0
Old Dependency Ratio	9.94	Beds per 1,000 pop.	2.2
Public Health Spending (% of GDP)	1.08	Public Education Spending (% of GDP)	1.94
Doctors per 1,000 pop.	2.5	Life expectancy	82.3

| Mobile Telephone Users per 100 pop. | 290.9 | Male | 78.9 |
| Broadband Subscribers of Internet per 100 pop. | 44.4 | Female | 85.6 |

Taiwan

Area (sq. km)	36,179	Population Density (persons/sq. km)	646
Capital City	Taipei	Currency	NT $
Total Rainfall (mm)	2,061	Av. Temperature (°C)	24.1
Total Sunshine Hours	1,272	Av. Humidity (%)	72

Economic Indicators

GDP (NT $ billion)	14,981	Origins of GDP (%, 2012)	
GDP ($ billion)	503	Agriculture	1.68
GDP per head ($)	21,558	Industry	30.00
External Trade of Goods ($ billion)	575	Services	68.32

Social Indicators

Population ('000)	23,374	Pop. Growth Rate (‰)	1.85
Labour Force ('000)	11,445	Unemployment Rate (%)	4.2
No. of Households	8,286	Av. No. per Household	2.8
Children Dependency Ratio	19.3	Old Dependency Ratio	15.5
Health Spending (% of GDP)	6.6	Public Education Spending (% of GDP)	3.7
Health Personnel per 1,000 pop.	11.1	Life expectancy	79.9

TV households (% with cable)	84.4	Male	76.7
Telephone lines per 100 pop.	52.6	Female	83.3
Mobile Telephone Subscribers per 100 pop.	127.1	Broadband Subscribers of Internet per 100 pop.	32.2

Notations

—	nil or negligible
¥	RMB yuan, Chinese Renminbi
$	US Dollar (unless otherwise stated)
HKD	Hong Kong Dollars
NT $	New Taiwan Dollar
MOP	Macao Pataca

Notes

Figures in this book, unless otherwise indicated, refer to the year ending December 31, 2013.

Abbreviations

bn	billion (one thousand million)
cu. m	cubic meter
kg	kilogram
km	kilometer
GDP	Gross domestic product
GNI	Gross national income
m	million
SCE	standard coal equivalent

Glossary

Balance of payments is the record of a country's transactions with the rest of the world. The current account of the balance of payments consists of: visible trade (goods); "invisible" trade (services and income); private transfer payments (e.g., remittances from those working abroad); official transfers (e.g., payments to international organizations, famine relief). Visible imports and exports are normally compiled on rather different definitions to those used in the trade statistics (shown in principal imports and exports) and therefore the statistics do not match. The capital account consists of long- and short-term transactions relating to a country's assets and liabilities (e.g., loans and borrowings). The current and capital accounts, plus an errors and omissions item, make up the overall balance. Changes in reserves include gold at market prices and are shown without the practice often followed in balance of payments presentations of reversing the sign.

CPI (Consumer price index) measures the changes over time in the price level of consumer commodities and services generally purchased by households. The year-on-year rate of change in the CPI is widely used as an indicator of the inflation affecting consumers.

Crude birth rate refers to the number of live births in a calendar year per 1,000 population of that year.

Crude death rate refers to the number of deaths in a calendar year per 1,000 population of that year.

Debt service ratio is debt service (principal repayments plus interest payments) expressed as a percentage of the country's earnings from exports of goods and services. The **liability ratio** is debts expressed as a percentage of the gross domestic product of the current year. The **foreign debt ratio** is external debts expressed as a percentage of the country's earning from exports of goods and services.

Child dependency ratio is the number of persons aged under 15 per 100 persons aged between 15 and 64. The **elderly dependency ratio** is the number of persons aged 65 and over per 100 persons aged between 15 and 64. The **overall dependency ratio** is the number of persons aged under 15 and those aged 65 and over per 1,000 persons aged between 15 and 64.

Economically active population refers to the population aged 16 and over who are capable of working, are participation in or willing to participate in economic activities, including employed persons and unemployed persons.

Registered unemployment rate in Urban Areas refers to the ratio of the number of the registered unemployed persons to the sum of the number of persons employed in various units (minus the employed rural labour force, re-employed retirees, and Hong Kong, Macao, Taiwan or foreign employees), laid-off staff and workers in urban units, owners of private enterprises in urban areas, owners of self-employed individuals in urban areas, employees of private enterprises in urban areas, employee of self-employed individuals in urban areas, and the registered unemployed persons in urban areas.

Final consumption refers to the total expenditure of resident units for purchases of goods and services from both the domestic economic territory and abroad to meet the needs of material, cultural and spiritual life. It does not include the expenditure of non-resident units on consumption in the economic territory of the country. The final consumption expenditure is broken down into household consumption expenditure and government consumption expenditure.

Import and export of goods refer to exported goods through Chinese customs. Both import and export of goods are valued at free on board (f.o.b.) prices. Free on board prices can be regarded as the purchaser's prices paid by importers when claiming goods at the border of the exporters. When the importer claim the imported goods, the goods have been loaded in importer's carriers or other carriers, and the exporter has paid export duty or received export redeem.

Import and export of services refer to services provided between resident and non-resident units, including services on transportation, tourism, communications, construction, insurance, finance, computer and information, consultancy, advertising and publicity, as well as film, audio and video services, royalty for patents, trademarks and other special rights, other commercial services, and government services.

Foreign direct investment refers to foreign investment in China through the establishment of foreign invested enterprises, cooperative exploration and development of petroleum resources with domestic investors and the establishment of branch organizations of foreign enterprises. Foreign investment can be made in forms of cash, physical investment, intangible assets and equity, in addition with reinvestment of the foreign enterprises with the profits gained from the investment.

GDP (Gross domestic product) refers to the sum of all output produced by economic activity within a country. GNP (gross national product) and GNI (gross national income) include net income from abroad e.g., rent, profits. For a region, it is called as Gross region product (GRP), or regional GDP.

Life expectancy refers to the average length of time a baby born today can expect to live.

Narrow money (M1) consists of cash in circulation and demand deposits (bank deposits that can be withdrawn on demand). "Quasi-money" (time, savings and foreign currency deposits) is added to this to create broad money.

Natural growth rate refers to the population change over a period as a percentage of the population at the beginning of the period.

R&D activities refer to creative work undertaken on a systematic basis so as to increase the stock of knowledge, including knowledge of man, culture and society, and the use of this knowledge to devise new products/processes/applications and improve existing products/processes/applications. R&D activities usually carry an appreciable element of novelty or innovation and can be conducted in such fields as natural sciences, engineering and technology, medical and health sciences, social sciences and humanities.

Total fertility rate refers to the average number of children that would be born alive to 1,000 women during their lifetime if they were to pass through their childbearing ages 15–49 experiencing the age specific fertility rates prevailing in a given year.

Sources

China Statistical Yearbook (2014), compiled by National Bureau of Statistics of China, China Statistics Press.

China Statistical Abstract (2014), compiled by National Bureau of Statistics of China, China Statistics Press.

International Statistical Yearbook (2014), compiled by National Bureau of Statistics of China, China Statistics Press.

BRICS Joint Statistical Publication (2014), compiled by National Bureau of Statistics of China, China Statistics Press.

China Statistical Yearbook of the Tertiary Industry (2014), compiled by National Bureau of Statistics of China, China Statistics Press.

China Statistical Yearbook for Regional Economy (2014), compiled by National Bureau of Statistics of China, China Statistics Press.

China Social Statistical Yearbook (2014), compiled by National Bureau of Statistics of China, China Statistics Press.

China City Statistical Yearbook (2014), compiled by National Bureau of Statistics of China, China Statistics Press.

China Labour Statistical Yearbook (2014), compiled by National Bureau of Statistics of China, China Statistics Press.

China Industry Economy Statistical Yearbook (2014), compiled by National Bureau of Statistics of China, China Statistics Press.

China Statistical Yearbook on Construction (2014), compiled by National Bureau of Statistics of China, China Statistics Press.

China Real Estate Statistical Yearbook (2014), compiled by National Bureau of Statistics of China, China Statistics Press.

China Security and Futures Statistical Yearbook (2014), compiled by National Bureau of Statistics of China, China Statistics Press.

China Environment Statistical Yearbook (2014), compiled by National Bureau of Statistics of China, China Statistics Press.

China Energy Statistical Yearbook (2014), compiled by National Bureau of Statistics of China, China Statistics Press.

China Trade and External Economic Statistical Yearbook (2014), compiled by National Bureau of Statistics of China, China Statistics Press.

Hong Kong Annual Digest of Statistics (2014), Census and Statistics Department, Hong Kong Special Administrative Region.

Yearbook of Statistics Singapore (2014), Department of Statistics, Ministry of Trade & Industry, Republic of Singapore.

Singapore in Figures (2014), Department of Statistics of Singapore, www.singstat.gov.sg.

Yearbook of Statistics (2013), Documentation and Information Centre of the Statistics and Census Service, Macao.

Statistics of Taiwan (2014), http://www.stat.gov.tw.

About the Author

Zhichang Liu, PhD, is an assistant professor in Chinese Academy of Social Sciences, Beijing. He got his MS and PhD from Institute of Political Science, Central China Normal University. He has been a visiting scholar at Deakin University for one year. His research interests are public services, grass-roots governance, and social development. He is the author of several research monographs, such as: *Basic Public Services in China: Changes and its Logic* (Beijing: China Social Sciences Press, 2014), *An International Comparative Research on the Basic Public Services Capability* (Beijing: China Social Sciences Press, 2014); and the co-author of *The Yearbook: The Public Services Capability of Chinese Cities* (Beijing: Social Sciences Academic Press, 2011), *The Public Services Capability of Chinese Cities* (Beijing: Social Sciences Academic Press, 2013). He has published 6 book chapters and 26 journal articles. Dr Liu also holds several research projects in the fields of public services, and urban grassroots governance.

Printed in the United States
By Bookmasters